Real Life Money

An Honest Guide to Taking Control of your Finances

By Clare Seal

KT-376-821

First published in 2020 by HEADLINE HOME
An imprint of HEADLINE PUBLISHING GROUP

2

Cataloguing in Publication Data is available from the British Library

ISBN 978 1 472 27229 4

Designed and Typeset by Avon DataSet Ltd, Alcester, Warwickshire

Printed and bound in Great Britain by Clays Ltd, Elcograf S.p.A.

Headline's policy is to use papers that are natural, renewable and
recyclable products and made from wood grown in sustainable forests.
The logging and manufacturing processes are expected to conform to the
environmental regulations of the country of origin.

HEADLINE PUBLISHING GROUP
An Hachette UK Company
Carmelite House
50 Victoria Embankment
London EC4Y 0DZ

www.headline.co.uk
www.hachette.co.uk

For E & O.
You are, and always will be, worth every penny.

Contents

Preface

**£25k of credit card debt. £2k of overdraft.
£0 accessible savings.**

On the 14th March 2019, I sat down and, with trembling
fingers, I set up an anonymous Instagram account under the
handle *@myfrugalyear*, with this as the bio. I had just finished
adding up what I owed, and it terrified me – I felt like there
wasn't space for it in my body, that I needed to channel it into
some external vessel, or it would consume me. I screenshotted
my spreadsheet, and nervously tapped out my first post,
imagining that I might gain a handful of followers who would
help me to hold myself to account as I tried to resolve this.

What happened next changed my life in a number of ways. It
rerouted my career. It changed my goals. It made me more
patient, kinder. It opened my eyes, and it made me check my
privilege. It put me in touch with the most amazing people,
and it gave me a platform. It's the reason I'm writing this book.

This book is for you if you've ever felt worried about money. If you have debt. If you struggle to save. If you live pay day to pay day. If there's always too much month left at the end of the money. If you're technically comfortable, but still terribly anxious. It's for you if you stop checking your bank balance on the sixth of the month, or if you're afraid to check it at all. If you wake in the night with the heavy weight of an unpaid bill sitting on your chest, or if you can never find quite the right time to discuss your money worries with your significant other. If someone's had to bail you out, and you're struggling with the guilt. If you find financial literature in general opaque, or smug, or intimidating.

It's not a prescription, or a one-size-fits-all plan for how to manage your money. It's not about getting rich quick, or aggressively paying off debt at the expense of all of life's pleasures. It's not about bullying yourself into frenzied frugality and then beating yourself up when, inevitably, you need to buy a new toothbrush on a 'no spend day'. It's not about making a promise never to have debt again, or to overpay on your mortgage, or to retire early. It's about gaining control of your finances, so that you are able to live peacefully with your past decisions, enjoy life in the present and plan for the future you want.

I hope that, as you read, you will see something of yourself in these pages. I hope you will realize that you're not alone. That everyone else isn't living an Insta-perfect life, free of financial stress, while you peer in through the Crittall windows, struggling to get by. That there are others whose lives and bank balances have been affected by redundancy, illness, addiction or loss. That you're allowed to feel angry about being let down by the benefits system or screwed over by childcare costs. That everyone else isn't making better decisions than you. That very few people are immune to the pressures of social media, and the temptations of relentless offers and promotions, the crippling expense of starting a family. That there's no need to be ashamed if you're not quite where you'd like to be, or even if you're nowhere near.

I hope that it will help you to rewire the way you think about money, to be kinder to yourself and to make better choices. To have the confidence to open up to your partner, friends and family, or to speak to your bank. To get to a place where you and your money can co-exist in peace. To reach your goals, but not at the cost of everyday happiness.

Your finances are fixable, but there are probably other things that need a little bit of mending first.

How did we get here, and is it really all our fault?

A huge part of this journey (I cringe at the word, but I've yet to find a better one) is unpicking the way we think and feel about money, our assumptions about other people, what we feel entitled to and the habits that follow. Ownership of our actions is vital for success in creating a better situation; I know, because I have spent years blaming external circumstances and waiting for things to change, and it has got me absolutely nowhere. The truth is, though, that usually the factors contributing to our own unique financial situations are myriad and complex, and not entirely our own doing. The political, social and economic climate, our background and upbringing, education and mental health all play a significant role.

So, while taking responsibility for our own part in things and identifying the behaviour we need to change is important, we also need to acknowledge that this problem is deeper and more profound than a simple inability to say no when faced with a 15-per-cent-off code or an invitation to a night out.

According to the Trades Union Congress, as of January 2019, UK average household debt stood at a staggering £15,400.[1] This is clearly a bigger issue than too many holidays, haircuts and houseplants.

Austerity has had a devastating effect on household finances generally. For those of us raised during the comparatively bountiful late nineties and early noughties – i.e. 'millennials' – the financial landscape we have had to navigate in adulthood is nothing like the one we were promised and prepared for growing up. We are priced out of the housing market. We have more debt than previous generations. Our wages have stagnated. The careers that once offered job security and competitive wages – teaching, emergency services, anything in the NHS – no longer offer that stability. A veil of despondency has fallen over many of us, because what's the point in saving if we'll never be able to afford a house, or if we'll have to work until we die, because we can't afford to save for a viable pension? In an era where there doesn't seem to be much of substance within our grasp, the instant gratification of a mini-break or a slogan T-shirt is infinitely harder to resist.

As Ben Elton would say, 'a little bit of politics there', but it's important to recognize that we're usually not the only ones to blame.

Why this book, and why now?

You may be asking yourself why I've chosen to write about this now, while I'm still very much in the middle of paying off my debt, rather than in a couple of years' time, when what I owe is all but a distant memory. During my (not infrequent) bouts of imposter syndrome, when my brain rounds on itself, I ask myself why on earth anyone would want to hear about matters of finance from someone who, at the time of writing, still has over £20k of credit-card debt. Is it not deeply hypocritical? Is it not the blind leading the blind? How will people respond to a book that is being written on a five-year-old laptop that will only charge when closed, resulting in a sort of perverse, enforced time-management technique that actually hampers productivity? Or, as I prefer to think of it, a unique incarnation of Hugh Grant's thirty-minute method in *About a Boy* – just without the playboy lifestyle to match.

Certainly, writing this from a place of solvency, with a bank balance firmly in the black, would be a far more comfortable experience. It would save the awkward, stilted conversations with extended family members, where I try to explain what I'm writing, and why somebody thought it would be a good idea to give me a book deal. It would be far more straightforward to say, 'Well, actually I had a lot of debt, but it's all paid off now, so I'm writing a book about how I did it,' than 'I've been in the shit, financially, for quite some time now, and I'm only just starting to turn things around. I started an Instagram page to hold myself to account, and it turns out that quite a lot of people feel the same way, so I'm writing a book to help us all get on top of our finances.' Quite the mouthful.

There is an assumption, which I shared until quite recently, that you have to be in serious financial difficulty to experience money anxiety or insecurity, but that couldn't be further from the truth. I want this book to be for everyone who has a less-than-perfect relationship with money – whether you have big debt, or whether you just find it all a bit baffling and want to start feeling in control. I want it to be for anyone who has ever felt a jolt in their stomach as they glance at a bill, or felt the need to lie when relatives enquire about how saving for a house deposit is going, or struggled to stick to even the most meticulously planned budget.

Holding off until my debt was clear would also have saved the difficult-to-navigate subject of book advances and how that might have affected my circumstances. (I'll get in there early and say: not much at all. While I don't think I need to disclose the exact sum, I'm happy to reveal that it was significantly less than the sum of my debt, and will be paid in four tranches – the first of which I've not yet received as I write this chapter.)

Despite all of these complications and uncomfortable conversations, I concluded that there is a plethora of books where people recount their past failures from a distance and – inspiring though they often are – I didn't want to sit down in front of my computer to write about this, only to find that my access to these emotions had long expired. As someone who has given birth to two children, I can attest to the fact that the human psyche is quite quick to forget pain, and I have come to realize that it is usually when you allow yourself to be vulnerable in the moment that you are of the greatest help to others. I felt that this book should recount the journey in real time, with all of the lumps and bumps that are often smoothed over with the passage of time and the fickle nature of memory, like a big pair of psychological Spanx. I knew how important those peaks and troughs would be to somebody in the same situation – that the minutiae count when it comes to matters of money in real life.

One Small Change

I realize I've already made a bit of a song and dance about how this book isn't prescriptive, but if I could give you one instruction before we start, it would be this: stop saying 'I'm in debt', and start saying 'I have debt'.

It's a fairly small shift in language, but I've found the removal of the verb 'to be' transformative in how I frame the situation in my mind. 'I am' is, by its very grammatical purpose, definitive, and hints that there is a permanence to the situation that can make it seem completely insurmountable. Saying 'I have' doesn't let you off the hook, but it reframes the debt as something that's simply one aspect of your life, rather than part of who you are as a person. It also makes the whole thing a hell of a lot easier to talk about, which is a key part of this process, so I'll be referring to what we owe as 'having debt', rather than 'being in debt' throughout this book (apart from in direct quotes from other people and in articles).

Stop defining yourself by your financial situation. You are so much more than your debt.

Part One:
Fixing the Foundations

There are so many ways in which our relationship with money can be broken. Everything from our background and family history to our mental health and use of social media can play a part, and in order to create a lasting change in both our attitudes and our bank balances, we need to be able to go to the root of the problem. We need to consider what it is that has shaped our attitude and our habits, and look at what needs to happen in order for them to change.

In the first part of this book, you'll find hardly any numbers. What you'll find instead are insights, anecdotes, observations and questions devised to help you to understand why money isn't easy to deal with in the context of a real, busy, complicated life – and how we can make things better.

One
Broke, Not Poor

I have been broke. Not in a Carrie Bradshaw 'I'll just sell all my Manolos, and my boyfriend will buy my apartment' kind of way, but in very real, panic-inducing, life-limiting kind of way. I have spent weeks in an unplanned overdraft, twitching every time my phone rang and unable to open a letter without first trying to peer in through the address window in order to steel myself for the contents. I have had long periods of paying essential living costs with a credit card, biting the insides of my cheeks when something needed to be paid by BACS, or in cash. I have had to ask my family for help again and again, never revealing the full extent of the problem, borrowing just enough to cover the absolute essentials.

I'm not poor, though. Let me explain.

For two terms that are often used interchangeably (see also: skint), there is a notable difference between what it means to be 'broke' – just about managing with little disposable income, big debt and no assets – and what it means to live in real poverty, where you might be skipping meals to ensure that your children are fed, or unable to heat and light your home in winter. I have no experience of the latter, and I recognize how privileged that makes me. I know that, if push came to shove, there are people who would put a roof over my head. I have friends and family who would help me to keep the wolves from the door, and for that I am eternally grateful. Broke is easily fixed, in relative terms. The climb out of poverty, in a country where social mobility is dying faster than any trendy houseplant I've ever owned (RIP), is a lot more complicated, and I'm in awe of anybody with the grit and determination to manage it.

Recognizing that I begin this journey from a place of privilege is important. Our backgrounds shape so much of our relationship with money, and our fundamental understanding of how it works, so that by the time we are adults, our financial instincts are often sewn inextricably into the fibres of our identity. We identify ourselves as 'good with money' or 'bad with money', as if that defines who we are as people, and isn't part of a more complex combination of our character, our upbringing and our circumstances. So often that definition of ourselves can become a self-fulfilling prophecy, pushing us to make decisions that perpetuate those labels. It's the voice telling you to buy the shoes, even though you've got a similar pair, because you're 'in debt' anyway – or, conversely, to save that easily affordable bus fare although your feet are aching, because you can't be certain you won't need that money for something else later.

I've always been a spender. When we were kids and my sister was given money, she would save it, whereas I would be itching to get out to the shops to buy whatever Beanie Baby I'd had my eye on. The buzz of a new possession has always been a huge draw for me, always scratching an itch, but never for very long. Delayed gratification has never really been my thing.

Throughout my teenage years, my experience of money was split definitively into two camps, divided along the line of my two households. My parents had divorced when I was a tiny child, and both had remarried within a few years. I saw my dad every weekend, alternating Friday night only with Friday and Saturday nights. Often, on a Sunday afternoon, I would break away from whatever book I was reading, or film I was watching, to find him, lying on his bed, scribbling columns on a blank piece of paper in his minute, neat handwriting. As soon as I entered the room, he would hurriedly slide it back inside its plastic wallet, tucking it neatly back into his sock drawer before engaging in conversation. It was only years later, looking back, that I realized that they were sums, and that he must have been working out his budget. He had never had money growing up and, although he was now living fairly comfortably on a senior teacher's salary, frugality was his way of life. Meals were simple, and usually home cooked. We borrowed books from the library, things were mended rather than being replaced, and going shopping would never have been considered a leisure activity. He wore the same clothes until they quite literally fell to pieces. One of the only times I ever saw him argue with my stepmum was because she'd tried to throw away the T-shirt he'd got for completing the Three Peaks Challenge, on the perfectly reasonable grounds that it was now more holes than fabric. He had a forest-green fleece that he wore when it was cold, and when I imagine him, it is zipped up right to his chin, his hands shoved in the pockets with his Ventolin inhaler and his Midland Bank change-bag full of coins. I don't remember ever seeing him use a credit card, and we never really discussed money beyond a few stilted conversations about how I, as a teen working part time at The Disney Store, couldn't really afford to spend with reckless abandon.

He died when I was twenty, and left me £10,000. I spent it, mostly, on a solo trip to Bali, where I tried to figure out who this new, fatherless version of me was. I ate banana pancakes, trekked to the monkey temple and went to surf school. Sounds totally *Eat Pray Love*, right? But I also got an inner-ear infection so bad I couldn't even keep water down for days, got lost in some rice fields, spent four hours trying to find my way back to Ubud and got my surfboard leash tangled around a dead, waterlogged cow that was inexplicably floating in the ocean. Luckily, I didn't get Instagram until 2012, so this trip went largely undocumented.

I have never felt so out of orbit as I did in those years following his death, and I still get a pang when I imagine what he would think of some of the decisions that I made during that time. A good deal of my money shame comes with an imagined raise of his thick, dark eyebrows – the wordless gesture of dis-appointment that would make my heart sink as a child and teenager. I often think of how much easier things might have been, had I done what he would have done with the money, and saved it for a rainy day, but a large part of this process has been coming to terms with the fact that I simply cannot change that. I have read so many accounts of people having trouble dealing with inheritances, and it seems that frittering away money that a loved one has left you is probably one of the most human things you can do. I was angry with him for dying, and I was angry with the money for not being him. I think, somewhere deep down, I just wanted it gone.

My mother's attitude to money was very different. She is one of the most generous women you could ever wish to meet – so generous, in fact, that she rarely manages to keep anything back to sustain herself. My parents separated when I was a baby, after which I lived primarily with my mum, just the two of us at first. She remarried when I was seven, and my new stepdad was, in a word, rich. After my sister was born, we moved from our cosy, terraced house in a working-class suburb of Birmingham to a massive, four-bedroomed detached house about a forty-minute drive away, in the greenbelt. I hated that house. The driveway was so big that it had a roundabout in the middle. It had tiled floors, garish wallpaper and a death trap of an unfinished spiral staircase, with a metal bannister painted in green. The garden was huge and very beautiful, with a magnolia tree that draped over the patio. But the whole place was the dominion of my stepsiblings and it was steeped in their memories. It's the house where we got a dog, where I first logged in to Microsoft Encarta, where I cried in the bath because I didn't want to go to grammar school. I drive past it, very occasionally, and feel nothing. I don't really remember the descent into financial difficulty as my stepdad's first, then second, business failed. I was too young to equate the disappearance of his buttercup-yellow Lotus or the talk of selling up with money problems, and when we did move into a smaller, rented house, I found I liked it better.

After we left the big house, my mother and her husband started a business together, in her field of expertise rather than his, and the ebb and flow of money became as tangible within our house as any piece of furniture. There was either an abundance or there was none, but every time things started to get really hairy, a big invoice would be paid, and it would seem that the building itself breathed a sigh of relief. The frequent trips to Pizza Express would be reinstated, and life would continue as before. I would hear snatches of conversation about loans and trips to see the bank manager, but I never worried too much, and when, aged eighteen, I needed to replace the brake pads and discs on my car, I took out my first overdraft.

When I started university and opened my student bank account, I ticked the boxes for an interest-free overdraft and interest-heavy credit card on the application form. I absorbed the extra £2,000 of my overdraft into my ideas about how much money I had to spend. I had fully excavated it in a matter of months, despite my maintenance loan and a generous allowance for living expenses from my family. I'm still in it now.

The first time I wrote all this down, solid black lines started to appear, connecting the dots between how things were growing up, and my behaviour now as an adult. I recognized that the reason I felt able to remain wilfully oblivious for so long was that I was waiting for that bail out, always assuming it would come. And it usually did, in the form of some birthday money, or a utilities refund, or, in more difficult times, in the form of help from family when I was forced to admit that I was struggling.

When I first left university, I was earning £16k per year on a punishing hospitality schedule, feeling that I was entitled to treat myself to whatever material possessions I desired because I was working so hard. My rent was almost half of my monthly salary, and I was spending the rest with reckless abandon – mostly to impress other people, or to try to make up for what I felt I was missing out on, working such antisocial hours. I got into a cycle of using payday loans, promising myself each time that this was the very last one, only to swiftly realize that there was no way to make it through to the next pay day without borrowing again. Some respite came in the form of family members giving me a place to stay, rent free, for a couple of months while I got back on my feet – but I still didn't get it. I plateaued at a sort of kneeling position, and I still had no idea what it was to live within my means.

My husband and I met at university, and started working together after our final exams, both opting to stay put rather than heading home – Birmingham for me, Newcastle for him – or to London. It took us four years of friendship to start a relationship, and four weeks of dating to accidentally start a family. In my naiveté, money was not really one of the myriad things that I panicked about when we learned of this unplanned development in our future. I worried about work, sure, but I had no idea of the impact that statutory pay would have on our situation, and I continued to ignore the warning signs long after our eldest son was born. We stumbled through the years that ensued, always saved just in the nick of time by a new job with better pay, or a bonus, or a family bailout. My husband had some terrible luck with jobs in the hospitality industry, where the hours are often punishing, and the bosses are often feckless, but looking back, I'm not entirely sure that this even really contributed to our financial situation. We could have managed through the crossover periods, had we had a handle on things, but we were clueless.

A Pinterest-perfect wedding and a second baby later, things started to spiral out of my control. I managed the finances in our family, and the more I let them slide out of my grip, the less I felt able to be open about our situation with my husband. He was still (and is still) working long, antisocial hours, at the expense of his health and happiness, and we were desperately struggling to make ends meet. We would skirt around the issue, allowing it to come to the boil with increasing frequency, but always somehow muddling through, and never really changing anything. I still feel the tight grip of shame on my heart when I think of the frivolities – the scatter cushions, the seagrass baskets, the Insta-famous houseplants – that cost our family its financial stability for that period of time. It's something that I am having to prise away, finger by finger, by making better choices and allowing time to elapse. It's hard to forgive yourself for what you perceive to be weak moments, but it's an essential part of the process of healing your relationship with your finances.

There's something about recounting my story that feels somewhat self-indulgent, but my reason for sharing my path to this point is not to wallow, or to make a point about how I am somehow a 'better' person now, in the style of the sort of self-help book that you might find on Bridget Jones's shelf. It is simply to acknowledge how I got here, the mistakes I have made – there are many, and I have plenty more to share – and to tell you that I know we don't all begin from the same starting line.

Privilege

There are many different opinions on the validity of 'The Privilege Walk'[1] as a method for teaching children about the socio-economic factors that often dictate the shape of someone's life, but I find it an excellent demonstration of the concept that I'm trying to pinpoint. The exercise usually takes the form of a race, with a cash prize at the end. Participants are lined up, and then instructed to take steps forward and backward, depending on whether a set number of statements, for example whether they have divorced parents, apply to them. Once the statements have concluded, some participants will be within a few steps of the cash, whereas some will be meters away from even crossing the starting line. As a physical manifestation of an idea that is very difficult for some people to grasp, I find it incredibly powerful. It also helps me to understand the shame that I feel, as somebody who was born within reaching distance of that prize, but who now finds themselves on the floor with a sprained ankle, all because I got distracted by something shiny.

Both of my parents went to university and worked in professional jobs, and I would consider both my upbringing and the life I lead now to be solidly middle class; by and large, there's always petrol in the car and hummus in the fridge. I am acutely aware, however, that skipping back even one generation demonstrates how socially mobile both sides of my family have been. My maternal grandmother grew up in a tenement in Greenock, near Glasgow, sharing one room with her parents and three brothers. She is a sensational woman, who came to England at nineteen, almost seventy years ago, and hasn't lost one drop of her musical Scottish accent. I was brought up on her tales of the poverty they suffered, but also of the warmth, togetherness and sense of fun that held their family together. I would drink in her soft, gentle voice, recounting the real-life 'meet-cute' of her first encounter with my grandfather, allowing it to feed my whimsical, romantic spirit. It seemed to me, throughout my childhood and well into early adulthood, that money couldn't possibly be as important as, say, love. I suppose that demonstrates a tendency in my character to sweep over the difficult bits and focus only on the loveliness. I can't quite decide whether that's such a bad thing overall, but it's certainly left me unprepared for areas of life that require a higher degree of pragmatism.

Of course, I now realize what a privilege it is to have been able to grow up in a socially mobile family, where the ground was prepared for me to go forth and make a success of my life. Where there would always be someone to catch me if I fell. Not everybody is that lucky.

In fact, some people of my generation are the catchers – they are the ones who have broken out of childhood poverty to earn well, often supporting their own parents throughout their adulthood. I've heard from a number of people for whom the feeling of shame of growing up poor – in itself completely proof of the fact that our money shame is often not entirely logical – has endured even once they've found relative financial security. Something I like to do frequently on my Instagram account is to ask questions, and share the answers. All of the replies detailed in this book have been shared with the permission of the person who wrote them, and I hope they will help you to see just how common it is to have a less than healthy relationship with money. Whether or not I recognized the feelings and behaviour described myself, patterns would emerge and my inbox would be flooded with people saying 'I thought it was just me'. When I asked about money shame, one person responded:

I was born in a squat and now earn a very good salary but feel bad for my parents. I pay their bills and for other things (I used to live in Australia and would pay for their trips out there) but I never really feel like I am not the really poor girl who washes her clothes in the bath.

The woman who wrote that response was kind enough to discuss things further with me, in an exchange that helped me to understand a whole different kind of relationship with money and work. Her frank words about what it's like to make the transition from relative poverty to a position of wealth will stay with me for a long time – the way in which it has affected her relationships with everyone in her life, and with herself, is very moving. If ever there was a testament to how intrinsic money is to our experience of life, this is it:

It's not easy to explain how having money after growing up without it leaves me feeling on a day-to-day basis. It's always made me feel 'other'.

The first difference is that my parents have no money. My brother and I pay for their bills, and at Christmas we buy my dad his annual supply of shower gel, or something basic like that. They live in poor conditions, and not having jobs (both are on disability living allowance for various long-term illnesses) has removed them from the society that works, meaning they have no friends or interaction with greater society.

Most of my friends are from very wealthy backgrounds, and I think I earn more than most of them – by at least double. When I got to university, I was so excited for there to be more of a level playing field – I thought that everyone would be skint – but the reality was that, at my uni, most people had their rent paid by their parents. That was when I realized that even though we were adults, the financial backing of my fellow students' parents, and the silent blanket of confidence this gave them, would stay with them throughout their adult life. It was hard to recognize that I would never feel that.

It's put a strain on my relationship with my parents in more ways than one. In the past my mum has said to me that I look down on her, which upsets me more than I can explain. I really, truly don't look down on her, it's just that such a big part of me wanted to be comfortable and wanted the security of money.

So I am in this odd in-between place of never feeling like I am the same as my friends from different backgrounds, but I also don't feel the same as my parents anymore because I live so differently to them.

In terms of my relationship with money and how I spend, I find it easier to live on less money but there have been other consequences. When pay day comes, I spend a lot – trying to pay for happiness for my parents, and clothes to try to get rid of the feeling that I am judged for how I look. I think this comes from being poor at school and never feeling that I looked the same as everyone else.

I worked so hard and smart to try to break through the poverty barrier and to feel like I belonged by having money, but it hasn't worked. I grew up poor enough to know that the phrase 'money doesn't buy you happiness' is only said by people with money. I have realized that not having it is everything, and having it is nothing. You just find other things to worry about – earning more, buying more shit, saving more. It doesn't fix anything.

It also has become more complex since I had my daughter, a year ago. Right now, she's small enough to be oblivious, but I really fear the day when she starts noticing the difference between my parents and my husband's parents. I am so fiercely protective of my family that this new family world I have created scares me. My daughter is also going to have things I never did, and sometimes I get mixed feelings about the future that I am going to provide for her. Is it jealousy? Is it fear that I will spoil her? Is it feeling like she will have such a different childhood to mine that we will be so different that we won't be able to relate? I don't know.

Perhaps I will never feel quite right, but I'm trying to make peace with it. I now tell people that I grew up poor, and am almost proud. It used to take about a year and a bottle of wine for me to confess my 'dirty secret', because I felt ashamed that I grew up so poor, and that I had so little money compared to my friends. I used to try to buy the guilt in our differences away, but I now do it as a nice thing to do. It's probably the same outcome, but the feeling of guilt is gradually lessening.

Through it all, I know if I lost my job tomorrow, I would clean toilets for a living until the end of my days if I needed to. My upbringing taught me to be a grafter, and I am finally proud of that.

As someone whose journey has taken me in somewhat the opposite direction, it was eye-opening to see how emotive the subject of money could be, even for people who were completely financially solvent. As I'm quickly learning, simply getting more money is very seldom the answer.

Education

Only now does it strike me how bizarre it is that, by and large, it's left to our parents to teach us about money, and how to manage our personal finances. I certainly wasn't taught it at school – unless you count my larger-than-life form tutor, telling us a story about how she had taken out a store card to take advantage of the discount, but then cut it up as soon as she got home and paid it off straight away. I, along with thirty other blank faces, had no clue what she was talking about without context from the wider curriculum, and it was quickly forgotten in favour of some of her other antics. I now know that she was talking about how to avoid paying interest, of course, but you could argue that it's a little too late for me. She lives a few doors down from my best friend now. I kind of hope she doesn't read this book.

Having parents who are free of their own money hang-ups, who can equip us with the skills and, let's face it, the financial support we need to get off to a good start is a very rare privilege. Which isn't to say that everyone else has rubbish parents – mine were/are wonderful – just that this vital life skill is somehow not given the same weight in child-rearing as, say, breastfeeding, baby-led weaning and limiting screen time. So, either we get lucky – our parents are shining beacons of financial excellence, who guide us just enough to empower us to take control of our own finances, while also factoring in the unique economic challenges of each generation – or we're left to find our own way. When you think about it like that, perhaps it's not so shocking that so many of us struggle. Maybe it's not all our fault?

Your debt is not your character

I think that, to an extent, your natural character dictates the way that you interpret situations, and the way that you react to them. Try as I might to be pragmatic, I can only usually manage a brief period of realism before my inner fantasist distracts me with daydreams of kitchen islands and trips to the Maldives. I know that upon hearing my grandmother's story, a different child might have absorbed a different message, and resolved to live a simpler, less materialistic life – because if you can have a happy childhood sharing a few square feet with five other people, then surely you can survive without a Dyson Airwrap. This is how I explain how siblings can emerge from very similar childhoods with completely different goals in life, and it's been an important step for me in absolving myself of some of the guilt I've had to face when embarking on this climb. That other version of me might not have had the optimism to battle through university while being eaten alive by grief, or survived a year in a provincial Italian town, where the main language was a thick dialect – of German. Such a large part of untangling our fragile, complex relationship with money is reliant on being able to accept our past decisions and, ultimately, who we are as people. To acknowledge that making different decisions going forward doesn't mean we have to waste our energy on berating ourselves – rather, that we simply need to try to understand ourselves better. We don't have to change our personalities, but perhaps we can change the way we react to certain triggers. Relieve some of the pressure that comes from living in a world where our every success is to be captured and immortalized on social media.

There's a reason that it's not as simple as just 'not spending', after all. Re-evaluating our relationship with money forces us to do more than just look inside our wallets or bank accounts. We have to look inside ourselves. We have to think about what it is that we value and how we want to spend our time on this planet. Who we are. Who we want to be. What's important to us.

We need to get to know ourselves, and accept all parts of our character. Even the part that spent £42 on a baby gro. But that doesn't happen overnight. We are talking about fundamental change here – not of our personalities, but of our mindsets.

The more accounts of money management that we can read and recognize, the less alone we will feel. The looser the grip of that shame becomes. In June 2019, I read an article for *Stylist* magazine by author and journalist Poorna Bell, whom I have long admired thanks to her seemingly effortless way with words, and her absolute strength in the face of adversity. The piece was subtitled 'Why we need to talk about our money f**k-ups', and it was one of the first things I'd seen in a mainstream publication that made me feel like a normal person. She wrote:

> *I work a lot in the space of addiction, and there is a strange parallel between that and money, in terms of how we moralize it.*

We assign values such as 'good' and 'bad', with no
acknowledgement that a person's 'bad' relationship with money
isn't necessarily because they are selfish or irresponsible, but
instead dependent on what they were exposed to as a child.
And in the same way that we believe sobriety is the cure to
addiction, we believe that simply having more money can fix
our issues with it.[2]

This was one of those penny-drop moments for me. It was
when all of the thoughts I'd been having about how complicated
personal finance really is compounded. I finally realized why I
was having to look in so many different places in my life to find
out why my relationship with money was so awful. Because
it's not as simple as 'bad with money = bad person' and 'good
with money = good person'. We are not defined by what we
earn, what we own, or what we owe.

Real Life Money

We all have a different past, different motivations and different
susceptibilities, but, as long as we continue to live in modern
society, we all need to learn how to live with money – how to
decide what's worth our hard-earned cash and what isn't, how
to make those micro-decisions every day, how to deal with the
emotional fallout of a credit-card blowout or an unexpected
bill. We need to learn to navigate social media without that
gnawing sensation of inadequacy. To take the carefully styled
and edited photographs, passed off as a breezy everyday snap,

for what they are: a carefully curated highlight reel, where all of life's drudgery is piled up on the other side of the room, behind the camera. That endless scroll of high-exposure, low-saturation beauty can make even the savviest person question their whole life, and look at what they need to buy in order to bring it up to scratch. We need to accept that our financial decisions are not a reflection of our value as people, and acknowledge that, in the end, there are far worse things that a person can do in their life than spend too much money.

I'm not here to absolve you, because no absolution is required. Whatever poor decisions you've made, no matter how much debt you have, however secret you've kept your struggles, there is a way forward. I hope I can help you to see it. I hope that this book will help you to understand the reasons why you feel the way you do about money, and to see what steps you can take to reframe your finances in the context of your life. To feel less alone. To let go of the shame and guilt, and make a plan to go forwards, unburdened. Your goals may even change during the course of reading the book, as mine may during the course of writing it, and that's okay too.

After all, you've got other shit to worry about.

Two
What are We So Ashamed Of?

Guilt and shame. What a pair. They often coexist in a swamp of self-loathing, in a corner of our mind that we visit frequently when plagued with financial difficulties. Difficult though they are to extract from one another, they are actually two very different emotions. I'm going to attempt to explain them in an effort to help us to shed them – or at least shrink that swamp down to a manageable size, maybe put up some flood barriers. A crocodile net or two, perhaps, but I'll stop short of any Steve Irwin references. In order to get real with our finances, it's absolutely vital that we understand these feelings and develop the tools we need to combat them when they inevitably come creeping in, unbidden, and risk derailing any progress we've made.

I'll start with guilt. Fun fact for all you fact fans: in German, the word for 'debt' and the word for 'guilt' are the same. Make of that what you will, but it implies something of an assumption that there can be no debt without guilt – that the very action of borrowing is laden with negativity and must weigh heavily upon your shoulders until you set it right.

I often think of guilt as a precursor to shame – the moment where we choose whether to act or whether to allow whatever is bothering us to become baked in over time, turning slowly into something more chronic. Because they relate to an action, feelings of guilt can be fleeting and are generally easily assuaged, if you're willing to face those uncomfortable thoughts when they arise instead of squashing them down. Take, for example, those times when you buy something you know you can't afford. You get it home and the guilt kicks in. If you choose to return it, the guilt is alleviated, and you forget about it pretty quickly. If you choose to keep it, you probably don't enjoy it as much as you would otherwise, because the guilt remains. When you're £30 short for a bill and have to let it bounce or ask for help from a family member, that guilt turns to shame. You probably won't notice all of this happening, at least not in an active sense – as has been the case for the many times I have done this – but it is there all the same.

The crucial thing to understand here is that, under the right circumstances, guilt can be useful. It can tell us that something we've done doesn't sit comfortably with our idea of who we are (or who we want to be) and, as long as we know how to process it, it can help us to correct the mistake and make better decisions going forward. When we ignore that little alarm bell, we risk internalising that guilt, and compressing it down into hard, hot shame. We stop believing that the problem is the action – the mistake – and convince ourselves that the problem is ourselves.

I tried to approach this chapter as though it was going to be possible to discuss guilt and shame without quoting heavily from Texan 'Queen of Vulnerability' Brené Brown, but the fact of the matter is that she explains these feelings with such pitch-perfect eloquence that anything I might try to formulate myself feels somewhat clumsy and contrived in comparison.

In her second TED talk after the viral 'The Power of Vulnerability', entitled 'Listening to Shame', Brown was able to articulate this vital distinction between guilt and shame in a way that actually makes sense:

> Shame is a focus on self, guilt is a focus on behaviour. Shame is 'I am bad.' Guilt is 'I did something bad.' How many of you, if you did something that was hurtful to me, would be willing to say 'I'm sorry. I made a mistake?' How many of you would be willing to say that? Guilt: I'm sorry. I made a mistake. Shame: I'm sorry. I am a mistake.[1]

Similarly, Brown is able to capture what shame feels like, at least to me, down to the very last detail:

> [. . .] the best way to describe shame, to me, is shame is this – the feeling that you would get if you walked out of a room that was filled with people who know you, and they start saying such hurtful things about you that you don't know that you could ever walk back in and face them again in your life.[2]

The fact is that the stigma of debt and financial difficulty provides precisely the right conditions, as identified by Brown, for shame to thrive and grow: secrecy, silence and judgement. Secrecy: keeping the situation from our friends, family members, and sometimes even our partners and ourselves. Silence: the inability to talk openly about how well or badly we're managing, even when we really need to offload. Judgement: the fear that if we let go of the first two, we'll have to read our own disappointment in somebody else's gaze too.

There have been times, over the past couple years, when I have felt the full weight of £25k's worth of shame descend on me. I have let it completely drench me, filling my pockets and pooling around my ankles, making me doubt whether I have anything of value to offer to anyone who matters to me. Shame is an emotion that's so difficult to deal with, we can seemingly only handle short, intense doses of it. It might always be there, hovering in the background, but we ignore it as we hand over our Amex on the morning coffee run, as a self-preservation technique. It tends to pounce when we're at our most vulnerable. When we're already feeling tired, or upset, or lonely, it can launch out of the water like a crocodile, tightening its limbs around us and rolling over and over until we submit. But sometimes, if we wade out to meet it, if we examine some of those feelings in greater detail and actually speak them aloud, we are better able to identify what's true, and what is simply our minds playing tricks on us.

There are books, podcasts and academic papers dedicated in their entirety to shame, why we feel it and how we tackle it, so I've no hope of delving fully into its grimy depths here. But money, spending and debt are subjects that are so thoroughly steeped in shame that it's difficult to imagine being able to discuss finance without a twinge of embarrassment or regret, no matter what your circumstances are. The things we feel ashamed about range from having spent irresponsibly to not having savings, covering a plethora of perceived fiscal mis-demeanours in between.

It's worth noting that a little bit of shame is simply a side-effect of humanity and empathy. Where we feel we have privilege, where we have acted selfishly, or where we have let someone down, as is inevitable over the course of a normal life, we carry a little shame with us. When it becomes a problem is when that shame becomes life-limiting, and that's what we're trying to tackle here.

There is a common narrative in 'redemption' stories (where someone overcomes their demons and goes on to become a 'better' person) that the act of hitting rock bottom is often the only propeller back towards the light. You'll find it in addiction stories – anyone who's read Russell Brand's autobiography can attest to the fact that these pivotal moments are often described in vivid, graphic detail – or any number of American debt-repayment testimonials, where debt is often linked to morality in a way that is both unhelpful and more or less entirely false. Here, shame is positioned as a motivator to be 'good', rather than 'bad'.

I don't buy it. In fact, my very issue with shame is that it's not productive – and any action that it does incite is usually fuelled by self-hatred and punishment, rather than a desire to take positive steps forward. There is no amount of shame that can enforce meaningful, lasting change. Moreover, once it sets in, simply changing the situation causing the shame isn't always enough to remove it.

Shame also makes us make bad decisions. Our reluctance to discuss subjects that are a source of shame for us massively reduces our capacity to seek advice and solidarity from those who would be able to really help us, isolating us from others in the same situation. It leaves us feeling around in the dark for the best solution. This is how payday loan companies and poor credit lenders, with their absurdly high interest rates and less than stringent lending criteria, thrive. They lurk in the shadows, jaws wide open, waiting to catch those who think this is their only option. If I'd had the good sense to confide in almost anybody about the struggles I was having post-university, there's just no way I would have ended up in the payday loan cycle. I probably still had a reasonable credit score back then and, to be honest, somebody would probably have just lent me the cash (there's that privilege again). I didn't owe a lot, but the shame weighed just as heavily on me with a few hundred pounds worth of debt as it did with tens of thousands. I was too ashamed to admit that I couldn't manage my income and outgoings, and I only turned to family as a last resort, when I got stuck in a cycle of borrowing that my meagre salary couldn't keep up with. Even then, I told people only what I absolutely had to, and didn't ask for the help that I needed with understanding how to balance my books. Because I was ashamed.

So, not only is letting go of shame absolutely essential in helping you to live a good life while you're sorting out your finances, it's also pretty important in getting you back into the black too. You're far more likely to get the best help if you can be honest with your bank about what you're struggling with, and you're less likely to feel the endless pressure to keep up with friends and family if you can share the reason you can't go out for bank-holiday drinks. The relief that comes from not bearing the burden of financial difficulty alone will make such a difference to your everyday happiness and wellbeing, I promise. We'll talk about how best to open up a little later on, but for now, allow the idea to percolate as something you might just be able to do in the future.

Common types of money shame and how to handle them

In order to help you to reframe and let go of the shame around money in your own life, as I'm learning to, I'd like to explore some of the specific forms that shame often takes when it comes to money, and how we can try to release ourselves.

Much of this is about identifying where we have made mistakes, but choosing to learn from the outcome, rather than internalize and perpetuate that spike of pain we get when we acknowledge what we regret saying, doing or not doing. I hope it will help you to see that anything you might have done, any money you might have spent, wasted or borrowed, shouldn't condemn you to a lifetime of self-loathing.

This is important, so don't skip this bit – you'd be surprised how much of it probably applies to you.

The shame of being an ostrich

I know the HSBC customer-service telephone number off by heart, but not because I call them so often. I know it because, for a very long time, I couldn't bring myself to answer the phone to them. Even if I knew I needed to speak to them that day, I would let it ring out, needing to buy myself that extra couple of hours to armour up before calling them back to discuss why my account was incurring penalty fees. My heart would pound as I saw the familiar digits spring up on my screen, and I would silence the vibrations and turn my mobile over, then delete the voicemail to avoid the unbearable red-circled '2' in the corner of my phone app. I have a theory that people who leave voicemails are a special breed of sadist anyway, and I already knew what it was going to say.

I have filed letter upon letter in a groaning drawer of my sideboard, never to be opened. Again, I knew what they said – had been waiting for them to drop on to the mat, in fact – but I just couldn't bear to see it there, in black and white on letterheaded paper. And I would know that things were particularly bad if, rather than the single sheet of paper telling me that 'we were not able to make the payments you arranged', the envelope was thicker, indicating the presence of a Money Worries booklet. It probably wouldn't have hurt to give it a read, but that sort of thing doesn't really occur to you when you're in ostrich mode.

One of the ways that I've tried to combat money shame and isolation on my Instagram account is by asking difficult questions and sharing the answers, like a sort of financial PostSecret. Every single time I do this, I get inbox Armageddon, with hundreds of people latching on to the particular answer that resonates with them, and telling me how much easier it made things to know they weren't the only one.

When I asked about shame, a popular response was that people were ashamed of the amount of time that they had managed to keep their head in the sand, or the fact that they still opted for a gritty face full of the stuff from time to time rather than face reality.

In the winter of 2009, I got a speeding ticket when my house-mates and I were singing along to Band Aid's 'Do they Know it's Christmas?' too loudly and enthusiastically for me to notice that the limit had dropped to thirty. The letter arrived at my student house just before I went away for the Christmas break.

I left it on the side in our communal kitchen in halls, and never picked it up again. I kept telling myself I was going to deal with it, putting it off even when my student loan landed and I could easily afford the fine. Then my dad died, and I stopped caring about anything much for a while. I was so determined to ignore it that, two years later, I found myself setting up a payment plan to settle what I owed after bailiffs turned up at my mum's house during my year abroad. The total was over £600, vs the £80-ish original fine I would have faced in the first instance. Looking back now, I really can't explain why, at twenty years old, I thought that it would just go away. The shame of this particular episode still snaps at my throat when I pass that speed camera. Some things are easier to let go of than others.

The thing worth remembering here is that ignoring problems is the most natural defensive reflex in the world. Sometimes you *need* to pretend everything's okay, because otherwise there's just no getting through the day. No, it's not healthy to spend years in denial, and I recognize now how massively my reluctance to face my debt has contributed to my anxious relationship with money, but it's difficult to confront a problem when you feel that you'll be powerless in the face of it.[3]

Since facing up to what I owe and starting the long journey back to the black, I've often let my mind wander back a couple of years, to a time when my debt wasn't at quite such an eye-watering level. I've thought about how easily solved it would have been then, if I'd just woken up and smelled the coffee when I had £5k, £10k, £15k of debt, even. But, crucially, I didn't. There isn't anything I can do to change that now; all I can do is be glad that my head is now fully sand free and make sure I resist the urge to re-submerge it as soon as things get a little tricky.

There's more about how to keep a calm and clear head when opening letters, listening to voicemails and picking up the phone to your bank and lenders later. For now, remember that having ignored letters and phone calls, or been unable to face up to the reality of your financial landscape for whatever period of time doesn't automatically qualify you for a public shaming on *Can't Pay? We'll Take it Away* (which should be removed from the air with immediate effect, but that's a fight for another day). You can stop this type of destructive behaviour without hating yourself for having done it in the past. Everybody has turned a blind eye to information they were scared of at some point.

The shame of earning well, and still having debt

If there's one myth that I've well and truly busted for myself, it's that financial security is dependent on earning more, more, more. For a long time, it was genuinely baffling to me that people my age, on a similar salary or less, were able to afford to save for a house, or simply live comfortably without debt. I assumed that they had significant help from their parents – and some may well have done – but I'm fairly certain that what set them apart was their ability to decide that they simply couldn't afford things, and to live within their means. (There is also, of course, the possibility that I didn't really know that much about them, and that they were swimming in just as much debt as I was.)

I would anticipate bonuses and pay rises as though they and they alone were going to make the difference, as though a bigger salary would somehow magically make me better with money. The reality is that, with each increase, our spending would adjust accordingly, and we would be no better off than before. In fact, lulled into a false sense of security by an increase in income, we were at risk of putting ourselves in even more jeopardy – taking on more commitments, and more debt.

This, of course, is reflected by lenders. The higher your salary and the more assets you have, the more credit they are willing to offer you (and the more tempting the interest rates) and the more debt you can accrue. As you may be able to tell, I don't really represent the typical readership of the *Financial Times*, but I was fascinated to see that in a recent article about financial wellbeing, their personal finance expert Claer Barrett asserted that 'You can have a successful city career and still be troubled by these questions – debt problems pay scant respect to income. The more you earn, the bigger the debts you can amass.'

She goes on to say that, according to the publication's Salary Finance Survey, almost one third of workers confessed to regularly running out of money before pay day and 'intriguingly, those earning over £100,000 reported the same level of concern about their personal finances as those earning less than £10,000.'[4]

Anecdotally, I have found this to be true. If you'd told me in March that my Instagram account would grow to be followed by tens of thousands of people and I'd be writing a book about the matter, I would have told you (after a brief lie down) that I assumed it would be mainly aimed at and consumed by people earning an average or below average wage. But I frequently receive messages from people who earn very large salaries, confessing that they are just as clueless as the rest of us. Often stuck in a lifestyle that they feel they need to maintain for appearances' sake, which is something that I can relate to on a fundamental level, they are trapped in a cycle of borrowing that can sometimes reach staggering amounts.

The years of chasing the pay rise that I was convinced was going to plonk us on a healthy rung of the property ladder – and fund an Aesop handwash in each bathroom – were closely followed by a period of chasing a bigger salary because I needed to – to keep up with the debt repayments. I knew that something needed to give, but my blinkered perspective meant that all I could see was: higher salary = more money. I didn't really think that we were overspending, not for how hard we were working. But I wasn't paying close enough attention.

So, it's really, really not just you. Overestimating what you can afford based on your salary is incredibly common, and it's perpetuated by lenders offering more and more credit as your salary grows, and peers seeming to have it all too. Like most things we're ashamed of, talking helps – you might just find that that friend or colleague whose life looks so enviable from the outside feels the same way as you.

The shame of not feeling like a 'proper' grown up

I turned thirty recently, and it had quite a strange effect on me. I've heard from others who have felt the same way – a sort of involuntary internal stocktake occurs as your life ticks through into a new decade, and it can leave you feeling raw and vulnerable. You start thinking about how you'd imagined life at the age you are now and, inevitably, about all the ways in which you don't measure up. As I sat on my sofa, looking at the row of number thirties winking at me from the mantelpiece, I suddenly felt a bit overwhelmed. Where was my three-bedroomed house, my glittering career, my financial security?

Then I took a second to look at the cards again. There was a 'Mummy' one. A 'wife' one. Countless from friends and family. It occurred to me that I had friends who were homeowners and were also single. Friends who had children and weren't married. Friends who were doing well financially, but renting. I realized that I didn't consider any of them not to be grown-ups because they hadn't ticked every box on that list of milestones – so why were my standards for myself so very different? Aside from the money thing, I actually appear to be quite a good grown-up, I thought.

The truth is that there are many other facets to being a functioning adult, but, for some reason, almost all of us put financial security in position number one when it comes to the criteria for grown-up-ness. I'm the oldest of my friendship group, and so far I've been the first to hit most of the major 'milestones' – first to get their driving licence, first to move away, first to have babies, first to get married – but, in spite of that, I look at my friends who own homes and can afford more holidays and I feel inferior. And that is not on them. That's on me, and possibly on society in general, depending on how deep you want to go.

The number of references to age that I see when discussing anything to do with money shame is astonishing:

> *It just feels like something I should have under control at 34.*

> *I feel a person my age (40) should be sorted out financially and that time is running out to get there.*

> *At 35 with a good job, I feel ashamed I don't have my shit together like everyone else.*

Because of the perception that debt is irresponsible, it seems there's an idea that it's more acceptable in your teens and twenties, or before you've settled down and started a family, at least. In her book *Open Up: Why Talking About Money Will Change Your Life*,[5] Alex Holder writes about how she and her friends would share their meagre salaries and money mess-ups, until the point where they all started to progress in their careers, have families and buy houses – in other words, until they grew up.

We all know that there is value to be found in other areas of our lives, but still the idea prevails that our 'success' at any given age is defined by our financial successes and failures. I read a message recently that made me realize how skewed my own perspective has been, because despite seeing how absurd it is from an outside perspective, I've often felt the same.

> I feel a failure. No matter what else I've achieved in my life, this one thing defines me.

We have to let go of this feeling that it's too late, otherwise where does that leave us? It's not too late to change our mindset, and in turn our prospects, no matter our age. There is always time to learn.

The shame of not having savings

Of course, it's not only debt that can make you feel like less of a successful adult. I've lost count of the number of times I've felt comforted by a friend or colleague telling me about money difficulties they were having, only to feel completely stupid when they followed it up with 'I mean, I had to dip into my savings.'

I realized the importance of this safety net when it was already too late – when my financial commitments and deeply ingrained spending habits already had my salary stretched to its absolute limit. Every time I would try to put some money aside, it would come to the end of the month – or sometimes the middle – and I would need to withdraw it just to stay afloat. I genuinely couldn't understand how people managed to do it – even when there was enough money in theory, it just never seemed to happen. As my debt grew, saving began to feel entirely futile, especially if I thought too much about interest rates. I'll talk more about how to deal with this in the second part of this book, but it's an attitude shift that I didn't manage to grasp until quite recently.

As I found with practically every type of money shame, it seems I'm in good company when it comes to my embarrassment about my lack of savings. Any time I've asked about savings on my Instagram stories, the responses have raised similar issues to my own; the constant dilemma of whether to save or pay off debt, and the struggle to build up any kind of safety net is more common than you would think:

> I feel I shouldn't be saving while I have debt – but not having savings caused the debt in the first place!

> I have no savings at all. We literally live from one month to the next hoping that nothing goes wrong – and if there's ever an emergency, it has to go on a credit card.

Not having savings made me feel deeply insecure. It fuelled my anxiety.

I have no savings. I'm the main breadwinner. If I ever lose my job, we'll be homeless.

The frustration and anxiety of the responses seemed to pour out on to the screen as I read, and I realized that the shame around not having savings can be just as all-consuming as the shame of having debt. It fuels the same feelings of insecurity – that feeling of precariousness that comes from knowing that there's no plan B.

There is another element to this, which is that with the increase in living costs and stagnation of salaries, saving is materially harder for most of us. According to a 2018 study, more than half of people in their twenties have little to no savings,[6] with insecure work and a lack of disposable income cited as reasons. Couple this with a less-than-perfect relationship with money, and it's easy to see why our savings accounts are full of cobwebs and regrets.

The shame of judgement and disappointment

For the most part, Brené Brown's room full of people talking about you exists only inside your head, but sometimes it filters out into real life, and you have to face judgement and disappointment from others. If you are an obsessive people-pleaser, like me, you will find the concept of this almost unbearable.

As I write this, my Instagram account is still completely anonymous, but it isn't the fear of what a few thousand strangers would think of me that keeps me lurking behind a millennial-pink circle. It's what the people who know me in real life would think. The family members who have bailed us out, still never quite knowing the extent of the mess we were in, and the friends who we've tried to keep up with for too long. As *@myfrugalyear* grew in popularity, I started to fear that someone would bring up the account in front of me and talk about how irresponsible or ridiculous the person behind it was.

The truth is that there are some people who don't get it – who will never get it. I can understand that if you've always had a straightforward relationship with money – if you've never had to fear your bank balance, never had a direct debit bounce, never had to pay for a food shop on a credit card – it might seem vaguely absurd that people find themselves with debt, or without savings. If living within your means comes naturally to you, you might simply not understand.

When you're harbouring any kind of secret, you carry with you that fear, that assumption even, of what people would say if they knew the truth. Sometimes, in conversations, your fears are seemingly confirmed by somebody talking negatively about people in the same situation, like in this example from my inbox:

*At least twice a month I find myself writing all of my debt
totals on a piece of paper (usually during work hours)
pondering and stressing over them.* [A brief interjection here
to say that I have done exactly this] *It's a weird exercise but
I have to do it when I feel consumed by my debt. I was at a
BBQ recently where a woman was explaining that she
dumped a guy because he was in debt, which led to half the
group expressing how you cannot trust a person with such a
huge amount of debt, that the guy probably has no future
and other outlandish remarks. I was devastated and it
confirmed my reasoning of not telling anyone the true extent
of my debt.*

My first thought upon reading this was that this situation
needed someone to be brave enough to speak up and say that
they had debt, and still considered themselves to be trustworthy,
with a bright future. My second thought was how many people
in that circle were probably reeling inside, even as they nodded
their agreement. It's these misconceptions that can only
be broken down by more people being open about how they
were able to afford their kitchen renovation, high-end furniture
and brand-new car. Otherwise, we all assume that everybody
is paying cash, which gives those without debt license to judge,
and those with debt a reason not to talk about it.

I'm the oldest sibling in my blended family and, as such, I've
often felt the need to seem like I have everything 'sorted'. I
have cringed at the thought of some of my more sensible older

relatives, all of whom I love and most of whom have helped me out financially in one way or another, reading the words: *I have over £25k of credit card debt.* I have imagined their whole perception of me as a good daughter/granddaughter/sister/mother crumbling into dust, imagined them writing me off as a silly girl with skewed priorities. I have worried that my husband's family will stop thinking I'm good enough for him. As I write this, I can feel the sizzle of anxiety across my diaphragm. I've asked myself if opening myself up to this is the right thing to do many, many times. But then I remind myself of everyone who has been in touch to tell me that they're in the same boat, and it convinces me that the more people with a voice and a platform who speak out about this, the less shame will surround the subject, and the more open we can all be. That's why it's worth the risk.

The shame of having to ask for help

The dry mouth. The racing heart. The hot cheeks. If you're anything like me, any bailout requests are usually in text form, as you just can't bear to hear the words tumble out of your own mouth, in your own voice. It feels like more of an admission of failure that way, somehow. Having to ask for help isn't something that comes easily to most people, and we're not just talking about asking for a hand with moving a filing cabinet, here. In asking to borrow money, we feel that we are admitting to having failed at being an adult (see above). We feel that we are burdening those who love us with the obligation of either parting with some of their own money or watching us struggle, knowing they could have helped. That isn't the kind of push-pull dynamic that anyone enters into gladly. We're so used to reading accounts of purportedly feckless relatives and friends who have borrowed money only to piss it up the wall, and we don't want to find ourselves in that camp when, a few months down the line, we're not in the position we thought we'd be in and can't pay it back.

And, of course, the truth is that when we're not in sync with our finances, we're unlikely to only need to ask once. Being stuck in the habit of spending beyond our means creates a cycle, whereby borrowing to cover a shortfall creates only a temporary reprieve. So we have to ask again, and, each time, the shame increases. That, in turn, makes us more reticent to discuss our finances, and in less of a position to see things clearly, and take control. We tell ourselves that we'll be able to pay it back one day, and we'll be 'absolved', but that can't happen until we break the cycle and that, in turn, is unlikely to happen unless we address this shame.

It takes a huge amount of courage to face this shame head on, because it involves frank conversation and an awful lot of vulnerability. The only real way to free yourself of this is to talk to the person who helped you out. I'll discuss this in greater detail later on, but, in short: if the bailout was a gift, thank them. Tell them what it meant to you at that time, and what you've learned since. If it was a loan, again, thank them. Then tell them your plan to pay it back. No more pangs of guilt when they call you. No more catching yourself when you're about to tell them about a small luxury you bought recently. No more shame.

Windfalls, inheritance and 'wasted' money shame

Some money is worth more than other money. This isn't a reference to the plummeting value of sterling against almost every other currency in the world (although seriously, WTF?) but about the value we ascribe to certain money in our lives, depending on its source and the intention with which it was given to us. I hear from people all the time who tell me that they once inherited or were gifted a large sum of money, only to watch it disappear, and then ended up with nothing to show for it. They tell me how ashamed they are, how the person who gave it to them would be so upset if they knew that it had been frittered away on incidentals.

When the £10k that I inherited from my dad cleared in my bank account, I was twenty-one. I was in my second year of university, and I wasn't really thinking about my future in any serious terms. I didn't consider saving or investing it. It didn't occur to me that it could help me buy a house one day, or help me out in any way that mattered. If anyone tried to advise me on what to do with it, I don't remember how the conversation went – and I certainly didn't heed it. What I did was book a trip to Bali, and buy even more clothes that didn't fit. The money lasted less than a year.

For almost a decade, the weight of that shame has been crushing. The idea that I could have taken his last gift to me, just months after saying goodbye, and wasted it, was excruciating. I didn't just feel ashamed of myself – I felt like he would have been ashamed of me. The more I struggled with money over the ensuing years, the more I berated myself for not having invested it in my future. Any time anybody told me that he would have been proud of me – when I graduated, when my sons were born, when I got promoted at work – I would perform a non-committal nod, but a voice in my head would give an immediate rebuttal. No he wouldn't, it would say. Because of the money.

I never questioned that feeling. To me, it seemed that it was just a matter of fact, and something that I had to live with. I never stopped to think that there were reasons why I treated that money the way that I did. As I've already pointed out, I have a natural tendency to be frivolous, but it's also pretty clear to me now that there were other factors at play. Considering and accepting those has been vital to unloading this, the heaviest item in my giant backpack of shame.

The first Father's Day after setting up the *@myfrugalyear* account was hard. Facing up to something that you've been trying to ignore for a number of years can be fairly brutal, and I was still feeling as though a layer of my skin had been removed. Everything was raw, everything hurt more, everything meant more. I poured out my feelings into an Instagram post:

[I felt] that I shouldn't still feel guilty about the fact that I didn't get to say goodbye, or that I spent my inheritance when I should have saved it, or that he would have been horrified to know the extent to which my spending habits got out of control. That being reminded, at this time of year, of how difficult it was to find a Father's Day card for a man who preferred Tolkien and hiking to football and beer. I've received a number of messages detailing how people have spent to cope with grief, or 'frittered away' an inheritance, culminating in a persistent feeling of guilt and shame. This is something that I'm still struggling with – something that sits a lot deeper than my debt.

I'd referenced Cariad Lloyd's incredible podcast, *The Griefcast*,[7] and she surprised me by jumping in with a comment. She'll probably never know how much it helped me to find peace with this element of my past. She simply wrote:

So common to struggle with things they've left you, especially money. You don't want it, you want them back.

The penny dropped, and I was finally able to stop beating myself with that particular stick, every time something came up where that money would have come in handy.

The fact is that it's really easy to just let cash disappear at the best of times, and the last thing that any of us are doing in the fog of grief is thinking about how to spend the money that has been offered to us as some poor compensation for the person we loved. The pressure to spend it on the 'right' thing becomes so intense that we simple can't decide, and before we know it, it's gone.

I've received messages from people who've had windfalls of tens of thousands of pounds – inheritances, winnings, PPI claims – that have seemed to disappear as quickly and easily as a fiver found in an old coat pocket. It's fairly well documented amongst financial psychologists that a sudden windfall is easier to spend than cash that you've spent time and energy earning, with up to 70% of people who suddenly find themselves with large sums of cash losing it within five years.[8] The retrospective guilt and shame that comes along with it can be intense, and embittering, but there is comfort in knowing that this, like so many of the behaviours we associate with irresponsible money habits, is fairly common. We all know about celebrities who go bankrupt, or lottery winners who end up back at square one within a very short space of time. One man did it twice.

It is, of course, impossible to cover every single source of money shame unless I want to publish this book in several volumes. These are just a few of the sources of shame that I've identified as being prevalent, both from my own experience, and from that of others who've confided in me. There are other, more specific sources of shame, like having to raid your small child's money box to buy milk (done it), lying to your colleagues about what you did at the weekend to seem like you can afford fancier leisure activities (done it), and telling someone their birthday present is 'on order' because you haven't been able to afford to buy one yet (yep, done that too).

It's rife. Wherever you find money, you will find shame – and as we've established already, money is everywhere.

Shame, self-flagellation and accountability: knowing the difference and keeping yourself in check

The main thing I want to drum into your head with a giant Acme mallet is that there is a very clear difference between shame and accountability. When we make ourselves accountable, we acknowledge that, yes, we may have fucked up slightly, but that same knowledge gives us the power to change things. To improve things. Shame keeps us in the dark, keeps us completely blind and immobile. It's about as useful in this as a springboard make of quicksand, and if we don't kick it to the kerb, we'll never be free.

Making yourself accountable can actually be really useful in reducing and even abolishing the shame you feel, but it's to be handled with caution. If you're already in an emotionally vulnerable state, accountability can quickly turn into self-flagellation, which only serves to intensify shame. It's important to stop that train of thought when it gets to 'I did X' and before it arrives at 'therefore I am Y'. It's okay to feel that you've made mistakes, and it's fine to regret them, but it's dangerous to extrapolate to the point where you feel that you deserve punishment, because, as we'll discuss later, punitive budgets don't work in the long term.

So how to tread that narrow ledge of accountability without plunging into the depths of self-loathing? As with many of the steps in this process, it takes practice, but you should find that as you get better at drawing a line between what you've done and who you are, it slowly gets more comfortable. Eventually, it becomes a habit. If, like me, you tend to shy away from criticism, facing your mistakes head on can be really challenging at first. I have a natural tendency to catapult straight from 'I'm doing okay in life' to 'I'm the worst person that ever lived', but acknowledging that there are reasons why I made the choices that I did, and knowing that I wouldn't make those same decisions now, has enabled me to take responsibility for some of my less proud moments. It won't surprise you to know that I have found writing about my money misdemeanours to be incredibly cleansing and cathartic, but you don't have to write a book or start an Instagram account to get that same level of release. All you need is a pen and a bit of paper, or even just to *say* it, to open your mouth and claim your mistakes out loud. Everyone makes mistakes – it is what you do next that makes all the difference.

Things to repeat to yourself

This is a series of mantras for those moments when shame threatens to take over. I have found that they help me to see the bigger picture, and to refocus my energy on to something productive, rather than pouring it into the abyss. You can think them, write them down or say them aloud – sing them, if you like (but maybe not in the middle of H&M).

- I am not alone.
- I accept help when I need it, and I am grateful for it.
- My finances are not my character; I am not defined by my mistakes.
- I am accountable for my actions. I can't change my past, but I can change my future.
- I am allowed to let go of this shame.

You Are Not Alone

I'm trying to remember a moment in my adult life when I wasn't worried about money, to some degree. I don't think I can. Obviously, not every waking moment of my existence has been consumed by it, but it's always been there, bubbling away under the surface, coming to the boil every so often. The impact of finance on mental health is something that's only really come to light very recently – beyond those debt consolidation ads from the '90s, where a sad-looking couple would shake their heads at one another in a darkened room, red-stamped letters strewn all over the table – but as I look back over the last ten years, I can see the dips and dents in my own mental wellbeing, shaped more or less exactly like a graph of my financial situation.

The anxiety of unpaid bills and the frantic transferring of minute amounts from account to account, the overwhelming sensation of trying to keep track of different credit cards with different minimum payments and interest rates, never quite knowing when a payment is going to be taken out and often just blindly hoping there'll be enough there to cover it. The tangled mess of it either consuming every thought in your brain, turning you into someone who is incapable of finishing a sentence without getting distracted, or causing a system overload that makes you disengage entirely. I've felt all of these things. My natural M.O. when dealing with problems is either to ignore them entirely, or obsess over every minute detail, with very little middle ground. Broadly speaking, that's how I've approached my personal finances since I was old enough to have a bank account. You could probably describe my accrual of over £25k of credit card debt as swathes of the former, peppered with sharp, painful shards of the latter.

For a long time, I thought that I was alone in this. That I was uniquely stupid. Uniquely incapable. I felt that if I admitted the full extent of my financial illiteracy to anyone at all, I would plummet in their estimations, down to a messy Tarantino-esque death, with all of the unnecessary gore and none of the pithy dialogue. I knew what I thought of myself, and of my own decisions, and I couldn't bear for anyone I cared about to feel the same way. Throughout an adolescence and early adulthood where I was unsure of almost everything else, from my appearance to whether or not I was funny, I was fairly certain that I was reasonably clever. My confidence in that fact had underpinned my identity since primary school, and it somehow felt like admitting I had no clue how to manage my money would undermine that. So I kept quiet, kept making the same mistakes, and grew lonelier.

I was convinced that anyone else in my situation must have some kind of 'proper' reason for having so much debt, beyond a penchant for scatter cushions and restaurants with tasting menus. I was saturated with guilt and shame. I needed some kind of outlet, but I was afraid to tell anyone I knew. I didn't want my friends and family to look at me differently. I felt I'd lied to them, projecting an image of myself as a responsible adult who was worthy of their love and respect, when underneath it all I was completely fallible – a fraud. The worse I felt about myself, the less I felt able to confide, and the deeper the debt became ingrained into my life.

I will never forget the night that my Instagram account started gaining traction. Not because of the trill of follow notifications, but because of the huge influx of messages. Lengthy accounts of similar situations to my own, words flowing in such a way that I could feel, hear, smell and taste the relief pouring out on to my screen. I sat up for hours, drinking it in. Feeling my breath deepen and my teeth unclench as I realized I was not the only one who felt this way, that there were abundant others struggling with similar levels of debt, for similar reasons. Guilt, shame and secrecy were, of course, a common theme – but every word I read lifted a few grammes from my shoulders, and fed my desire to open up more, in the hope of providing the same relief for someone else. Far be it from me to keep that catharsis to myself. Here's an example of the type of message I received during that first twenty-four hours:

> *I read your story right after bursting into tears in my kitchen at the £20k debt I have and the massive burden I feel on my shoulders. Despite my husband and I having good jobs, we have racked up the CC debt and live day to day tracking our cash in a spreadsheet. Despite our best efforts it never seems to reduce. Anyway, the point of my message is I found your page when I really needed it and I feel relieved to know that I'm not alone!*

I really hope that the fact that so many others out there felt alone in this comforts you as it did me. I hope that they show you how normal it is to be fallible, and that you are not somehow perverting the natural order by having overspent and then struggled to recover, rather than climbing the property ladder or paying into your pension, or starting to invest.

It is only by opening up about our challenges, failures and mistakes in real time that we can break this culture of expectation around what we should have achieved at certain junctures of our lives. Around what is 'acceptable' or 'normal' debt – a massive mortgage, for instance – and what isn't. How can we know what's normal amongst our contemporaries, if we're all too afraid to admit to having bought our remodelled kitchen on finance, or having put that all-inclusive holiday on a credit card? By keeping quiet, we run the risk of creating a culture where we're just comparing ourselves to glossed-over versions of our peers, while we ourselves paper thinly over the cracks and hope nobody looks too closely. We are afraid to show any vulnerability when it comes to money, often because we have a specific idea of how our lives and bank balances should be. As a generation, we knock back 'shoulds' like tequila slammers, absorbing them into our bloodstreams until we can no longer see what we actually have achieved, because our vision is crowded with things we don't have, and milestones not yet reached.

It's not all your fault

I will finish by asking you this: if debt is such a dirty word, then why are we faced with a deluge of adverts for credit products? If we're never supposed to take out credit, for fear of being accused of being greedy or irresponsible, if debt is such a guilty and shameful secret, then why is it legal at all? You do not have to be ashamed for having taken on debt, or not having saved enough money. It isn't a sin – in fact, it's not related to your morality at all. Managing your income, outgoings and credit is a skill, and it requires practise to get right, just like driving a car or playing the piano. Perhaps some people have more of a natural aptitude for it than others, but that is true of absolutely everything. There's no shame in not being able to sit down and play Chopin without a single piano lesson, and yet we berate ourselves endlessly for not automatically knowing how to handle our finances.

Be accountable, yes. Take control, of course. But don't be ashamed.

A note from Poorna Bell

Poorna Bell is an author and journalist. Her article for Stylist *magazine on debt shame struck a chord with me – it's astonishing how soothing it is to find out that someone you admire a great deal has faced the same adversity as you. This is the power of being honest about money.*

While I'm not in debt at the moment, I've spent the majority of my adult life in debt ranging thousands of pounds across loans, credit cards and overdraft. During this whole time I felt shame around my debt – whether that was the amount of debt I accrued, not being able to afford or keep up with friends who earned a lot more than me, or when I had to ask to borrow money in times of desperation from loved ones. A big part of the shame was that I felt I had no one else to blame but myself – and that's true to an extent. I was a reckless spender, and very often I would spend and completely disassociate myself from what I was spending – it was credit, so it wasn't 'real' money to me. But there were things that should've been done to at least give me a fighting chance of having a proper relationship with money, and that includes being taught about finances at school rather than something completely useless like learning how to make a Swiss Roll in Home Economics. Or when I went to university, my bank not automatically giving me an overdraft – which I literally viewed as free money. This led to a catalogue of disasters just getting further into debt, when I wasn't earning enough to pay it back.

When out of the blue, I was given a promotion at work and given a much higher salary, I finally managed to pay off my debt. And I thought that would be the end of it – but shame is a hard habit to break, and money remained something I was fearful around, and I hated talking about it. I was still trying to pretend it didn't exist so I still did things like not checking my bank balance, or getting in a cold sweat when my friend harmlessly asked me about how we were going to budget for a big holiday we were going on. When I finally opened up about being in debt, or the fact that money is a very emotional topic for me, I was amazed at how many other people felt the same way. Not just that, but letting go of that shame meant I had a healthier relationship with it. The biggest gamechanger for me was getting a financial empowerment coach for a few sessions. Initially I was worried about spending more money when I should be saving money but she actually has helped me save money in the long run, and most important: take control and change the shame narrative. I always thought I was 'bad' with it. But she helped me to undo some of the toxic ways I view money and how I handle it. That has helped me let go of a lot of the shame and fear and I don't know that I would've been able to do that on my own. Ultimately, addressing our issues around money and shame is critical for our mental wellbeing. I don't think we realize how much it is a cause of stress – not just the actual having of it – but how much brain space it takes up. I didn't realize it until I released some of the shame around it – and trust me when I say, it is very, very heavy. It's okay to let go.

Three

Money on Your Mind

What better way to follow on from shame, which I have seen described as 'the bedrock of psychopathology' (i.e. the cause a plethora of emotional issues), than to move on to mental health? While broader awareness around mental wellbeing has grown in the last few years, with widespread coverage in the media and a wave of support across social media, money often seems to be left out of the conversation entirely. Prominent voices in the mental health space, like Matt Haig, Bella Mackie, Bryony Gordon and even Prince Harry, have helped to break some of the taboos around some of the less pleasant antics of our brains, and people are beginning to open up about their own struggles. For some reason, though, the financial causes – and indeed consequences – of mental health difficulties are, at best, an afterthought.

Of course, poor mental health can affect anyone at any time, but it's difficult to deny that a complicated and cyclical relationship exists between what's going on in our heads and what's going on in our bank accounts. According to recent studies, people with a diagnosed mental illness are 3.5 times more likely to have problem debt,[1] while over 100,000 people with problem debt attempt suicide each year.[2] Language used in debt collection letters can be aggressive, intimidating and anxiety-inducing, and as our mental distress about money problems grows, our ability to handle the situation with a clear head diminishes.

Poor mental health makes thinking clearly more difficult, and money management suffers

Mental health suffers

Financial difficulty

Worrying about money contributes to poor mental health

An on and on it goes. It's hard to separate cause and effect, to draw a line between what we spend because of poor mental health, and how our mental health is negatively affected by difficult financial circumstances. In a lot of ways, it doesn't matter what came first – if we can manage to understand the relationship between how we feel and what we spend, we might just be able to start breaking that cycle. One of my biggest realizations was identifying that both my overspending and my inability to face my bank balance head on reached their peaks at times when I was neglecting my mental wellbeing, or when external factors were making me feel anxious or lonely. When I struggled to adjust to the change brought about by having my second child, I focussed on what I could change about the house I was now spending most of my time in, pinned to the sofa by a nursing baby, my thumb tapping PayPal One Touch far too frequently. When a horrible situation ahead of my return to work made me dread walking back through the door, I spent on clothes and make-up to mask how humiliated I felt. While my husband was working 90-hour weeks, I spent my evenings planning the wedding I felt we deserved but knew deep down that we couldn't afford.

Because mental health is such a complex subject, and my own struggles with it cover such a small part of the spectrum, I can only really speak to my own experience and that of those who have confided in me. For that reason I consulted with clinical psychologist Dr Emma Hepburn, whose Instagram account, *@thepsychologymum*, is a fantastic resource for mental health, with Emma posting evidence-based advice from her practice in the form of excellent doodles. She told me that money and debt are two things that often come up in her clinical practice, and that, in her experience, the link is clear:

There is an abundance of evidence that not having enough money can contribute to poor mental health: the stress of being in debt, worrying about paying bills and the worry and stress associated with other aspects of financial instability can contribute to mental health difficulties. However, aspects of mental health can also impact on our relationship with money in a number of ways. When we are feeling down, the feel-good hit of shopping can be alluring, as we search for things that make us feel better. For some people, this is a coping mechanism to lift their mood, but the short-term hit of shopping can be quickly wiped out by the long-term impact that overspending causes, and the guilt, worry and debt can be maintaining factors contributing to mental health difficulties. In addition a common contributing factor in anxiety and others mental ill health is avoidance, so we do not tackle the money problems building up so they become an overwhelming problem that can seem too big to tackle, contributing to our overwhelm and stress further.

The good news is that once we understand this relationship, it gives us something to work with. If we know that poor mental health can damage our finances, it stands to reason that by improving our mental and emotional wellbeing – by seeking the help that we need and healing right at the core – we can start to solve some of our issues with money too. In the same vein, if we can get to grips with our finances, we may be able to relieve some of the extra stress and improve our mood. For some of us, looking after our brain chemistry means slowing down, reframing our thoughts, sitting with uncomfortable feelings or talking to a friend. For others of us it means therapy, meditation or exercise. For others still it means medication. There's no right or wrong way to approach this part, but it's absolutely vital that we address it.

Anxiety, depression and money, money, money

In June 2019, I was diagnosed with generalized anxiety disorder. It felt odd after years sliding up and down the spectrum of symptoms, from persistent worry and a racing heart to chest pains, nausea and crippling intrusive thoughts, to finally have someone official give me a proper diagnosis. You don't get a certificate or anything, and sometimes I still question the validity of it. I wonder whether I really do have something that constitutes a 'proper' mental health issue, or whether I've just made a lot of stupid decisions and now have to worry about the consequences (but then I suppose that's what someone with anxiety *would* think).

When I am anxious, it often feels like a deafening whirring sound in my head and a tingly, electric sensation in my palms, wrists and chest. It's noisy and all-consuming. Paralysing. It stops me from being able to focus on anything meaningful – I struggle to concentrate on work, I'm bad-tempered and restless, but not productive. I feel like I need to do *something*, solve *some* problem, but the issue causing me to worry obsessively is often the one thing that seems completely impossible. So I'm tempted to search for something else to fix instead, as a way of winning back control over my wayward mind. For a long time, scrolling through Asos or Instagram was my go-to remedy, something to do with my hands and eyes, the perfect distraction. The excess adrenaline that my body had created would be channelled into the pursuit of the perfect purchase, and I would continue to buzz furiously until the eventual release of the 'thank you for your order' page. I seemed to have an incredible ability to invent or exaggerate some problem that could be solved by buying something – the walls were too bare, the baby's clothes were looking a bit small, that cleanser wasn't really working for me – and set about rectifying things as a proxy for what was really bothering me. My decision-making was skewed, to the point where, if you'd asked me, even moments after the confirmation email landed in my inbox, why I'd made that purchase, I probably wouldn't have been able to tell you. And in an increasingly frictionless online environment where all of my card details were stored, with my thumbprint providing the only barrier, I wasn't able to question, or even realize, what I was doing in real time.

The feeling of relief would last until I was next forced to think about money – a time period that became increasingly short as my debt grew – after which the anxiety would return two-fold, given extra weight by those familiar feelings of shame and buyer's remorse. It's easy to see how the restlessness that is characteristic of anxiety disorders might be temporarily quelled by this behaviour, but it's equally easy to see just how quickly it comes back round to bite you on the arse, especially once you begin to enter the realms of financial difficulty. Once your life starts to be materially affected by the aftermath of your coping mechanisms, once it's an unpaid bill or eye-watering credit card statement that starts to eat away at your mental security, it becomes more difficult to draw the line between what's anxiety and what's genuine concern. It's fairly normal to worry about money, and financial anxiety is often experienced by those who aren't actually living through debt or other difficulties, but this spiralling behaviour can quickly become a cyclone, a real mental-health shitstorm.

I find that a lot of the practices recommended for managing anxiety are also helpful in managing the compulsion to buy my way out of that knot in my chest. When I finally realized that the crippling dread and increasingly frequent intrusive thoughts weren't going to go away by themselves, I reached out to my local NHS mental health service. I was seen quickly, because I was less than a year post-partum, and found talking therapy to be very helpful. During those first couple of sessions, the therapist asked me about my reaction to intrusive thoughts – did I hold the baby a little tighter when I imagined dropping him as I walked down the stairs? Did I move a little further away from the kerb when an image of falling under the wheels of an approaching white van would flash before my eyes? The answer, of course, was yes. She explained to me that by reacting to those thoughts and feelings, I was legitimizing them, and that they were likely to come back again and again – meaning that I would have to hold tighter and tighter, move further and further away from the edge of the pavement. But that if I was able to sit with those uncomfortable images, if I was able to call them out for the lies that they were, their grip on my life would loosen. This is the basic theory behind Cognitive Behavioural Therapy (CBT), which is often used to ease anxiety and a whole host of other mental health issues, and I was referred for a course. The idea that I didn't need to immediately react to feeling anxious or panicky was difficult to get used to – our default responses to those feelings are not easy to overcome. But slowly, over time, I have been able to reach a point where, whether it's an anxious spiral or an intrusive thought that I'm facing, I can usually control the impulse to buy something to resolve it. Interestingly, I found for a while that I would get the same level of anxiety relief from making an extra payment towards a debt, or from combing through my budget for more things to cut out. But I have come to realize that this is really just as damaging – there were a couple of months where I paid off more than I could afford to, and ended up making myself more anxious as a result.

My favourite theory about anxiety comes from the author Matt Haig. He says that he has stopped viewing his anxiety as an illness, and started viewing it as an injury that flares up when he forgets to look after himself. I find this idea incredibly soothing, as someone who understands that I'll probably never be free of those anxious thoughts entirely – that I'll never be completely 'cured'. For me, being open and discursive about what is worrying me – particularly money – acts as a salve for the wound.

I've never been diagnosed with depression, though I suspect that I've experienced it to some degree, particularly following my father's death and the birth of both of my children. I recognize many of the symptoms when they're described to me – the apathy, the lack of connection, that dragging feeling of doing everything through treacle. The way that the prospect of deciding what to have for dinner or washing your hair is enough to make you want to weep. I'm aware how much deeper this goes, but even my relatively mild experience of low mood makes it clear to me how much that little lift, the little buzz of something new, might help, temporarily. A pinprick of light in the dark, a drop of colour in the greyness. In his 2013 TED talk, activist Andrew Solomon declared that, in his view, the opposite of depression is vitality, rather than happiness,[3] so it follows that any behaviour that could be described as hedonistic – which shopping definitely can be, in my experience – might feel like a temporary relief. Solomon's description of his descent into a deep depression is both eye-opening and heart-wrenching, and it brought me awareness of something I hadn't previously given an awful lot of consideration to – a quality of severe depression that may pose the most danger to one's financial position. It is the loss of meaning. The inability to care about the outcome of any of your decisions, the complete despondency. It is the idea that everything is already so awful, so unbearable, that you might as well spend money on something that might offer you a moment of happiness, or even just the ability to feel something. Dr Hepburn agrees that there are some qualities of depression that could easily contribute to money problems: 'In depression, cognitive skills including problem solving and decision making can be affected, making it even more difficult to tackle any financial issues head on.'

A study by the Money and Mental Health Policy Institute suggests that as many as one in four people with diagnosed depression also have problem debt,[4] while depression sufferers who were in financial difficulty were 4.2 times more likely to still feel depressed after 18 months.[5] These figures are so significant that I find the lack of awareness of them staggering, especially considering the abundance of consumer debt and the deteriorating condition of our mental health services. It's easy to see how this can become a dangerous downward spiral, and those suicide figures, although still alarming, suddenly start to make more sense. It is only by bringing this conversation out into the open – by enabling people to speak out about their struggles with mental health *and* money without fear of judgement, that we can begin to pour some light into what can be a very dark place.

One of my favourite people to talk to about mental health is my friend Ali, whom I met not long after starting my Instagram account. After surviving severe post-natal depression and feeling that she wanted to share her coping methods with others, Ali co-founded mental health journaling company The Positive Planner in 2017. Not content with just creating a product to help people to connect with their thoughts and work through periods of low mental health, Ali and her business partner also run workshops and keep up a constant flow of discourse on their own Instagram account. Ali is one of very few mental-health campaigners I have seen address the money question, and she has really helped me to understand some of my own complicated emotions surrounding spending. I asked her why she thinks the two are so closely linked:

> *I think when you're suffering with your mental health, you often feel 'less than', and this is compounded by envy of others who seem to have it all together. Spending money can give you the feeling that you're doing something to better yourself, and it gives you a big hit of serotonin, which can soothe your frazzled brain in the short term.*
>
> *It doesn't last, of course, and then the shame and disappointment in yourself rears its ugly head. When we're in a vulnerable state, mentally, this can actually lead to us pushing the self-destruct button – the lower our self-worth, the more we try to hurt ourselves in various ways. Driving ourselves further into debt is definitely an example of this.*
>
> *We might also, of course, take the opposite approach. I think some of my own spending habits often come from a place of self-empathy – I've been working hard and deserve a treat, or have been feeling awful and need a pick-me-up. It's incredibly complex, I think there are any number of reasons why we spend when mentally unwell.*

I recognize both of the behaviours Ali described – in fact, I could probably walk around my house and stick a label with either 'self-care' or 'self-sabotage' on it on each unnecessary purchase – and it's this understanding that has helped me to curb the desire to reach for my credit card every time I feel even just a little anxious.

Emotional spending: recognising your triggers and breaking the cycle

Once you begin to notice how connected your emotional and mental wellbeing are to your shopping habits and general ability to manage your finances, it becomes easier to understand why it's not as simple as just not spending – whether that admonishment comes from someone else, or from yourself. When you have debt, it's all too easy to look back at the sprees, the excess consumption and the frivolities and see only the action, not the context. It is only by identifying these catalysts, these feelings that bubble up inside us, creating a pressure gauge that can only be relieved by the 'add to cart' button, that we can begin to make real progress. Dealing with the root cause of the emotions, rather than trying to distract ourselves from them. Because, believe me when I tell you, they will always be there waiting once the shine of that new possession has worn off.

There are any number of emotional factors that might compel you to shop, including:

- Boredom
- Loneliness
- Rejection
- Low mood
- Anxiety
- Jealousy
- FOMO

- Work stress
- Tiredness
- Feeling Overwhelmed
- Grief

Or, conversely:

- Happiness
- Confidence
- Mania
- Feeling that everything is perfect, and you don't want to ruin the moment with thoughts of your budget.

Each and every one of these reasons – or any other trigger you can identify – is completely legitimate, and don't let your inner Piers Morgan tell you otherwise. I think we sometimes fear that acknowledging the reasons why we participate in certain behaviours is somehow 'letting ourselves off the hook', but truly, it's the only way to create the foundations of lasting change. Recognizing that we spend irresponsibly when we're feeling a certain way doesn't mean that we just accept that and continue on our path to financial strife, it means that we empower ourselves to deal with the emotion itself, even when that's easier said than done. In improving our mental wellbeing, we can also ease the pressure on our finances.

But how do we tell whether we're spending 'legitimately' or whether we're trying to solve an emotional problem?

I went back to Ali to ask her opinion:

I think that we can coach ourselves to ask a series of questions to check the intent of our purchases. Things like: 'Is it useful?', 'Is it needed?', 'Why do I want it?', 'Will I still want it tomorrow? In a year's time?'

It's about focussing our attention on our own habits and being more conscious in our decisions – which is something that actually applies to a lot of other areas when we talk about improving our mental wellbeing.

So, perhaps the best way to think of the process of emotional spending is not as a cycle, where one outcome necessitates another, but rather as a circuit, where we can install trip switches that stop us from overloading our brains and credit cards. By stopping as we make decisions and adding intention to our actions, we should be able to slow the process right down, and give ourselves the breathing space we need to spend consciously.

It starts before we've even entered the shop, typed in the URL or swiped up on the affiliate link. Here, we have to ask ourselves – how am I feeling? Is this the right thing for me to be doing right now? Am I prepared to enjoy this experience but walk away empty-handed? Am I going into this process with purpose, or am I trying to fill a void or scratch an itch? If the answer to any of these questions gives you reason to believe that things might get out of hand, it's best to step away, and think about what it is that is really bothering you. I have been known to get caught in an anxiety scroll because of something as trivial as the fact that I haven't brushed my teeth yet and my mouth tastes funny, or I'm wearing an uncomfortable pair of pants. Give yourself the time to work out what is really bothering you. This is difficult at first – it can feel forced, silly and synthetic, but it will quickly become your most useful habit.

If you do decide to browse, it's important to stay in tune with how you're feeling and step away if you start to get over-whelmed. I've come to realize that a lot of my purchases have come from a need to just *make it stop* – usually when I've been scrolling for minutes on end, and I find I'm on 1,000–1,099 of 3,000 products. Every single market is saturated with more products than anyone could ever want or need – the rails bulging with similar styles of top, the web categories over-flowing with vases and cushions. Once we lose the ability to objectively decide whether we need or even want something, it's time to get the hell out of there – whether 'there' is a physical shop or simply page 45 of your search results.

Your final check*point* is at the check*out*. Before you hand over your card or autofill your details, do an internal check*list* (I'm done now, I promise):

- Does the thing you're buying have a purpose? This doesn't have to be practical – it could serve a genuine emotional purpose too.
- Do you really want or need it? Dig deep on this one – is your justification for buying it real or fabricated?

- Can you afford it? That's not to say 'shouldn't you be paying this money off your credit card instead?' It's asking, will this purchase cause future damage to your mental health or finances? This is the crucial one – and often the most difficult to answer.

My final recommendation for addressing the complexities of an emotional spending habit is my most fervent: pick up a pen, or open your notes app, and write it all down. Many people, including myself, find writing to be incredibly valuable in processing those emotions. Keeping a journal of your spending habits and the related thoughts and feelings can not only help you to see patterns and develop coping strategies, but can be shown to anyone you are reaching out to for help, in the event that getting the words out is just too difficult. I'm a huge advocate of journaling in general – absolutely anybody can do it and, as much as I love a fancy bit of stationery, all you really need is a biro and some scrap paper. It doesn't matter about spelling or grammar, and your handwriting doesn't need to be neat – you might never even read it again, but the simple act of writing things down can lend catharsis and clarity. I find that it can often unboggle even the most boggled of minds.

Dr Hepburn agrees that keeping a written record of your emotional spending can be really helpful.

Although it can be difficult looking at your money situation, thinking about your relationship with money and what you spend and why can help you gain control over your finances –

*although sometimes you may need help to do this as the
relationship can be complex and difficult to work out. Recording
your spending can be daunting and scary, but it can often
help you too see where things are going wrong – and right – and
can help you to gain clarity on a way forward. Although it
can be very difficult initially, longer term it can have a positive
outcome and helps to breaks the cycle of avoidance, which
can contribute to a sense of overwhelm and feeling out of
control with money.*

Making permanent changes to our habits can seem really
daunting at first, but by making incremental changes, by
questioning our motivations and always bringing our decisions
down to what is important to us, we can start to replace toxic
behaviours with healthier ones.

Emotional shopper or shopping addict?

'Shopping addict' sounds more like something you might find
in an Instagram bio or on a slogan T-shirt than an actual
mental-health condition, but the damage that it can do to our
finances and wellbeing can be profound. At the time of writing,
compulsive shopping is not yet considered an addiction by any
official body, despite calls by sufferers and clinical psychologists
alike. This means that it is in danger of being trivialized, written
off as irresponsible behaviour. It is, however, increasingly
recognized by professionals that it shares some traits with
other addictive behaviours: the obsessive thoughts, the tempo-

rary high that comes from the 'fix', the guilt and remorse post-hit, and the cyclical nature of it all.[6] Perhaps unsurprisingly, Compulsive Buying Disorder is only prevalent in developed countries, where consumerism is part of the culture and credit is readily available. Credit cards facilitate reckless spending, because they 'separate the pleasure of buying from the pain of paying',[7] meaning that there is no immediate cost for whatever it is you've bought. The pain comes later – we know it's there, waiting, but we often prolong this period of denial by not checking our credit card balance, creating a void in which our anxiety can build, ultimately leading to further spending in an attempt to untie the knot in our stomachs. I'm often asked why, when I also have an overdraft, my focus is on paying off my credit card debt, and this is one of the most prominent reasons. I find that a loan or an overdraft still feels like real money in a way that my credit card limit just doesn't, and I recognize that I need to prioritize undoing the damage caused by delaying the consequences of my overspending.

Because there is no official disorder recognized by the British Psychological Society, it is both impossible to get an official diagnosis and difficult to know whether your own behaviour would be classed as having an 'addiction' to shopping. That leaves it up to us to examine our spending patterns and consider how much or little control we feel we have over them.

In a 2018 article for the *Independent*, professor of behavioural psychology Mark Griffiths makes an interesting comparison to the recognized condition of having a gambling disorder, which he terms as being 'arguably one type of compulsive buying'.[8] When I asked him why shopping addiction is not yet classed as a bona fide addiction, he cited a lack of high-quality studies as the reason:

It's taken thirty years for gaming disorder to be formally acknowledged, and there are dozens of high-quality studies on that. There is so little of an equivalent standard in the shopping addiction area (and the same goes for sex addiction, work addiction and exercise addiction).

The relationship between all of these behaviours are often as tangled and unending as a necklace that's been left at the bottom of your handbag for months on end, and unravelling them can take time and patience that we often don't feel we have. To extend the metaphor to its absolute limit, in the same way that somehow only mums seem to be able to tease out those seemingly impossible knots, it may be that we need some outside intervention in the form of medication or therapy.

A further complication . . .

As if the subject of mental health weren't complicated enough, there is, of course, another layer to this. Something that transcends individual experience and forces us to look at mental health as a societal problem. As we've already established, I am writing this book from a position of privilege – I am broke, not poor – but I don't feel that this is something that can be ignored.

The mental health crisis in this country is not limited to those of us living above the poverty line, those of us who may be stretched almost to our very limits, but for whom there is a safety net. It is not limited to those of us who have a voice.

The part of Andrew Solomon's talk that had me nodding so furiously I gave myself a headache was the part where he spoke about the socio-economic aspects of depression – the way that we see it as a middle-class problem, because we only recognize it in those who 'should' otherwise be happy. He is, of course, speaking about the situation in America, but his comments translate to the UK and beyond. He explains that those suffering poor mental health and depression because of poverty are far less likely to be diagnosed and treated, because the difficulties they are facing are often real and measurable – things like sub-standard living conditions and a continuous struggle to put food on the table. It becomes almost impossible to know where the line is between an understandable feeling of despondency as a result of being trapped in a cycle of poverty and clinical depression – or if it even exists at all.

Psychologists Against Austerity is an organisation whose mission is to expose the impact of austerity policies on the mental health of the nation, and their campaign focusses on five key 'austerity ailments':

1. Humiliation and shame
2. Fear and distrust
3. Instability and insecurity

4. Isolation and loneliness
5. Being trapped and powerless

Their briefing document goes into great detail about the impact of each of these elements on mental health, and is a heart-breaking read. It highlights the fact that all of the factors that have affected my own mental health and financial position over the years – all of the chapters addressed in this part of this book, really – are amplified for families and individuals facing unemployment, job insecurity, benefit cuts and in-work poverty. It delves into the feeling of societal shame and humiliation piled on to those worse off by the mainstream media, and how it contributes to mental illness in those living in poverty. It highlights a real need for change.[9]

The second edge to this sword is that good treatment is often eye-wateringly expensive, and the availability of mental health resources on the NHS is very much a postcode lottery. This is a problem for anyone experiencing financial difficulty, but particularly for those without any way of raising the funds they need for therapies that are either unavailable on the NHS, or that have a year-long waiting list.

I don't have a solution to these problems, because they are not an issue of personal development – they are inflicted on people from outside. My hope is that by speaking about this, by normalizing debt and shouting about the link between money and mental health, we can start to create an awareness of the fact that financial stability is vital for emotional wellbeing. And that that applies to absolutely everyone in our society, regardless of class, career, income or education.

Don't be scared to ask for help

When it comes to my mental health, I have always found it incredibly difficult to know at what point to stop trying to deal with everything on my own. How do you tell whether what you're feeling is simply justifiable worry about a legitimate problem or something deeper? 'At times it can be difficult to extrapolate between a normal reaction to stressful circumstances, and mental ill health,' says Dr Hepburn,

> Because of the complex interplay with your life circumstance and how you are feeling, this is not always straightforward to do. It can also be difficult to notice changes in yourself as often this comes on gradually. However, if you notice a change in your emotions or behaviour that appears to be continuing for more than two weeks and is impacting on your daily life, you should seek help – this can include disturbed sleep, lethargy, a change in eating behaviours, avoiding contact with people, feeling unable to do tasks, suicidal thoughts, withdrawing from hobbies and interests, feeling continuous irritability, anxiety, low mood or tearfulness. In fact, a change in your shopping behaviour for some people can also be a sign that your mental health is suffering. If you notice any of these types of changes or feel you are not managing it is worth speaking to your GP who can direct you to the appropriate services.

Despite the progress that's been made, reaching out when you're at a low ebb – or even recognizing that you've reached a point where you might need some intervention – can be really hard. Knowing where to get support if you are stuck in a cycle of poor mental and financial health is difficult – the thought of talking to my GP about money worries makes my eyeballs sweat even now – but there are so many places you can find help. I've listed some resources at the end of this book, but it can be helpful to make a few notes on how you're feeling ahead of any conversation. The worst thing you can do, if you feel stuck, is keep it all to yourself.

You are worthy of help, whether you feel the right approach is to improve your finances by addressing your mental health, or vice versa. Seek it out.

A note from Anna Mathur

Anna Mathur is a qualified psychotherapist who shares insights into our behaviour and tips for how to improve our mental health through her Instagram account and her online Reframing Anxiety *course. Anna has been a great support to me during this, both through her uncanny ability to post just the right thing at just the right time, and through direct words of empathy and encouragement.*

As the letters come and the debt builds, so does the treacle-thick sense of shame in the stomach. Secrecy and shame keep us stuck. We often engage in self-destructive behaviour in order to punish ourselves for the mess that lies in our dark corners. It feels hopeless, like there is no way out.

Imagine a big old house with a padlocked, neglected junk room. The dust is building daily, covering old, beautiful furniture with a layer of grey that distorts the colour and blurs hand-carved detail. Every now and again, the rusty padlock is unlocked, and the door open just enough to chuck in another moulding box, or broken item, but not open enough to survey the scene for it provokes too much emotion to be stuck between what once was, and what could be.

But there is hope. I promise. The hardest and the most life changing thing to do is to open the door, to turn the light on and let it flood in. To see the reality of what has grown in the dark. It might be ugly, painful, overwhelming. The light and the breeze whip the thick dust into the air. But in time, with help, the dust settles and each piece of furniture, each item can be restored. Distressed but not destroyed. Messy but not broken beyond repair. It's tiring, dust fills the lungs, makes your eyes feel gritty, but it won't feel like that for ever. As the dust is removed, the impact lessens.

Open the door. Get someone who cares about you to stand beside you as you turn on the light. All the feelings, the anxiety, the fear, the trepidation, the sense of hopelessness, they may feel overwhelming and all encompassing. But there are ways, means, support, strategies and compassion available for you. You are not the only one who has been in this situation, regardless of how the shame has made you feel otherwise.

You have a story. Debt wasn't something you proactively chose for yourself. It will have been a chain of events, and I bet you that if you heard the true details of everyone's debt story, you'd feel a wave of compassion for them. If I heard yours, I would feel that same wave. Your story is worthy of compassion, not shame. And as you work through your debt, and allow yourself to be supported in addressing it, you'll be able to access that compassion. Shame cannot reside where compassion lives. There is hope. But first you must turn on the light. But you don't need do it alone.

An important note:

Shortly after I started writing about debt, I was speaking to a good friend of mine who also happens to be doing a PhD in clinical psychology. She told me that it's widely recognized among mental health professionals that the feeling that poses the highest threat to human life isn't sadness, or anger. It's the feeling of being trapped, of hopelessness.[10] The feeling of being stuck in a situation or cycle that has somehow spiralled out of your control is so applicable to having problem debt that it's little wonder that just under half a million people experiencing it consider suicide each year.[11]

If things feel out of control to this point, if you're feeling like there's no way out – or worse, only one way out – I urge you to use some of the resources listed at the back of this book. All are free, and all of the services are experienced in dealing sensitively with people who are experiencing problem debt or poor mental health, or both. There is always a way up and out.

If you feel that you have reached a mental health crisis point, please call the Samaritans on 116 123. There are other resources for both debt and mental health listed at the end of this book.

Four

Under the Influence

In the same way that I can't say with absolute certainty that, without the invention of social media, Donald Trump wouldn't have been elected President of the United States, I can't be entirely sure that I would have fewer money problems if I'd stayed off Instagram and Pinterest. But I have a pretty strong hunch that it's the case. I've always been an 'advertiser's dream', so maybe they were always going to find a way to get me? I'm less of a fantasist now than I was when I was younger, but my natural inclination is still to be easily suggestible and perpetually dissatisfied with at least a hundred different things about myself. The reality is, though, that I don't watch an awful lot of live television, I don't listen to commercial radio, and I can last all of two minutes with a magazine before it's ripped out of my hands by a squawking child. This means that, without social media, the opportunities to advertise to me, low-hanging fruit (yuck) that I am, would be limited, and my bank balance might look significantly healthier.

The reason that my susceptibility to any form of social advertising is such a particular source of discomfort for me is that social-media marketing is my professional background. I worked as Social Media Manager and then Brand Manager for a luxury interiors company until early 2019, planning the very same types of campaigns that I was falling victim to myself. I was completely immersed, and I guess that one of the reasons I was good at my job was that I *was* the customer. I understood what made them tick, what would make them buy. I bought multiple things from my own company in order to try to recreate the influencer aesthetic. It wasn't until after I left that I began to see what a trap it was for me, how much I had bought into the lifestyle that I was promoting to customers. When I left, I moved on to a smaller brand that I felt was doing good things for women, but the pressure to sell in excess, mostly via social media, was even more intense, if anything. It felt at odds with what I was trying to overcome in my personal life, and as I began to think more about the potential impact of aggressive targeting on social media, I struggled to enjoy the role. I left after four months, partly for this reason.

My love affair with social media began when I set up a MySpace account in 2006. My friends and I would frequently post to the message board to ask for comments on our new profile picture, set our songs to something loaded with teenage angst and put fashion colours in our side-swept emo fringes in a very early iteration of 'doing it for the 'gram'. Since then, social media has undergone the most gargantuan of transformations. In under fifteen years, it has gone from a basic, mostly organic and chronological place to share to a complex and incredibly effective advertising tool, driven by algorithms that are constantly making tiny adjustments, tailoring our feeds and serving us personalized content. It has changed our experience of life so quickly, and so completely, that we never really had any chance of remaining unaffected by it. It dominates our conversations, it influences our politics, it affects our mental health – and it makes us spend. In the UK alone, revenue from social media advertising in 2018 was 2.8 billion USD.[1] That's about 2.3 billion in Sterling, and accounts for targeted ads only. It doesn't take into account the culture of picture perfection that Instagram has created, the groundswell of comparison that makes us vulnerable to other forms of advertising, or the fortune generated by influencer marketing.

Of course, there are things I love about social media. It is a place of common ground, a place where we can bond over shared experiences and where we can offer and receive support, no matter what the topic. It is increasingly a place where activism thrives, where awareness can be raised and where real connections can be made. It is a hotbed of creativity, and it's allowed small businesses to grow and thrive. I have seen first-hand what can be achieved by sharing on Instagram, and my experience of the platform, since I reframed the way I was using it, has been overwhelmingly positive. But we need to learn to take from it only what we need and enjoy, instead of absorbing all of the unrealistic expectations, and allowing them to rule our life offline. We need to learn to protect ourselves.

Keeping the comparison monster in check

'Comparison is the thief of joy'. 'Compare and despair'. 'Don't compare your behind-the-scenes to somebody else's highlight reel'. There are an abundance of mantras and inspirational quotes out there reminding us not to compare ourselves to others, but we just can't resist it. For many of us, our tendency to compare ourselves unfavourably to others robs us of the ability to see the positives in our own lives, and social media has amplified this a million-fold. It has given us unprecedented access to the lives of other people, from friends and acquaintances to influencers and celebrities, and our natural instinct is to compare and compete, often to devastating effect on both our self-esteem and our financial security.

The problem is that we can only compare our insides to their outsides; our deepest doubts with their proudest moments. You can never know what's behind the curtain; whether it's really the powerful Wizard of Oz back there, or a mountain of credit card debt. And, somewhat ironically, precisely *because* of the stigma and shame attached to overspending and debt, a lot of people simply don't tell the truth about it. I, for one, have definitely been the person posting about booking a holiday or buying a new sofa, knowing that if either of those things were to happen, it would be on credit. For all I know, somebody with the exact same problem might have seen that, thinking that if I could afford those things, why couldn't they? And so the problem perpetuates.

In the summer of 2018, my Instagram-fuelled overspending reached an absolute peak. I was on maternity leave, spending a lot of time scrolling on my phone while breastfeeding a tiny baby. I would look first around my rented house, with its missing furniture, gappy floorboards and sterile, white, silk-painted walls, and then to my Instagram feed, filled with an abundance of newly renovated kitchens and Loaf sofas, and feel woefully inadequate. We had moved into the house earlier that year, leaving a beautiful but damp flat, which hadn't felt like the right place to bring a newborn baby home to. The furniture that had comfortably filled our previous home left gaping holes in the new house, and the fact that we were still renting left a gaping hole in my satisfaction with our lifestyle and circumstances. In spite of the fact that we already had a lot of debt at this point, I wanted the Insta-perfect maternity leave, so I tried to buy it – all on credit, of course.

I thought I was being savvy, using my staff discount at the interior brand I worked for to buy beautiful, Scandinavian-style furniture and trendy accessories, always looking for a discount code if I shopped elsewhere, but the fact of the matter was that we couldn't afford any of it, at all. I thought I was being reserved, because I didn't buy absolutely everything I wanted, just a few bits here and there. But I struggled to comprehend that my own circumstances were probably wildly different to those of the new mums that I saw cooing at an organic-clad baby in a Stokke Sleepi cot.

Of course, I couldn't be sure that their high-end baby gear wasn't bought on a credit card too, and that is another danger of the Instagram dream. Unless we take a moment to think, and question it, it forces us to take everything at face value. We struggle to see that there might be other factors at play, and whether we're consuming content from an influencer we love, spying on a former classmate, or even keeping up with a close friend, we often don't know enough about their personal finances to assume that we should be able to afford the same. I would look at how hard my husband and I worked, and the fact we had managed to claw our way up from a joint income of £32k to more than double that in just a couple of years, and I would compare our circumstances to people I perceived to be our peers. Then I would tell myself that, if they could afford the lifestyle I coveted, we deserved it as well.

So, I bought the French Connection rug. I painted the chimney breast in our living room in Farrow & Ball Hague Blue (with permission from our landlords, of course). I ordered a fiddle-leaf fig that got lost in the post and then was clearly disappointed with its accommodation when it finally arrived, as it died a slow, tragic death in the corner of my bedroom, shedding one leaf at a time like the rose from *Beauty and the Beast*. I tried to start a 'lifestyle' blog, with the intention of giving myself some kind of creative outlet to keep my brain alive, meaning well, but, in hindsight, definitely using it as an excuse to buy more 'stuff'. My personal Instagram account at that time was awash with carefully composed photos designed to give an impression of a life that I definitely was not living. I was as guilty of feeding the comparison machine as anybody else.

I'm not sure whether or not I wanted to actually become an influencer, though I 'joked' a few times to friends about how a gifted mattress, like the ones that were seemingly being handed out to everyone with more than 20,000 followers, might be nice. I didn't think about the trade off, or what it's actually like to have thousands of people watching your every move, which, ironically, I have some idea of now. I just wanted a perfect life, and I wanted it so badly that I forgot to look at and appreciate what I did have. For a time, I let it make me shallower, more superficial, less interesting. The people that I like to follow on social media are the people whose content comes from a place of genuine passion and interest. I recognize now that my attempt was just a pale impression of a lifestyle blog.

I think it's fairly safe to say that, when it comes to overspending, the crux of our issue with social media is that we're somehow convinced that the carefully captured images we see on our favourite feeds represent real life – the life we feel we should be living too. If magazines and celebrity culture have a lot to answer for when it comes to breeding feelings of inadequacy, then social media needs to stand up and take a deep bow too. I'll talk about the problem with influencers in a little more detail later, but there is some groundwork that we need to put in before we can begin to enjoy the content on our social feeds for what it is.

The biggest, most important step that I took in dealing with my tendency to compare myself unfavourably with what I saw online was to unfollow everyone who made me feel like shit. In fact, when I started the new account, I followed very few people, and gave some thought to what I allowed on to my feed. You can call it avoidance if you like, but my general thoughts on the matter are that, if you identify that something makes you do or feel things that you don't like, or that isn't good for you, stop doing that thing. With absolutely no offence intended, your favourite interiors influencer is not likely to notice if you stop following them for a while, and you can survive without knowing which tiles they chose for their downstairs bathroom. If it's a friend or family member whose posts make you feel inadequate, the 'mute' function is perfect, as they won't be able to tell that you're not seeing their content. It doesn't have to be permanent either. And it just might give you the breathing space you need to stop with the constant comparison, and to realize that you're doing absolutely fine. It might help to remove the need to spend in an effort to keep up, and enable you to rediscover your enjoyment of a platform that can sometimes feel overwhelming and relentless in its carefully curated perfection.

When it comes to changing your relationship with social media and reducing its capacity to make you feel inadequate, you may find it easier to go 'cold turkey' and come off the platforms altogether, or to take a break for a set period of time. Short spells of distance from habits that are having a negative impact on your life have become popular in recent years – think 'Dry January', 'Veganuary' and 'Second-Hand September' – and people often find the positive effects continue long after the month is over. However, if either of these options feels too extreme to you, or you rely on social media for some very important element of your life – promoting your business or staying in touch with family, for example – here are a few ways to stay on social media without letting the comparison monster take over:

- **Do something real**

  The temptation to carry on scrolling even once you realize your social feeds are starting to make you feel like shit can be immense, but you will only start to feel better once you break away. Go for a walk in a location that hasn't been chosen purely for the blossom trees en route and leave your phone at home, or switch to flight mode. Call someone, or have a face-to-face conversation. Bonus points if you actually discuss how you're feeling, and why, because once you voice the reason that you're feeling compelled to compete, the spell often breaks completely. Read a book. Read this book, even.

- **Practise gratitude**

  I am a reformed gratitude sceptic. I'd always considered it a bit saccharine, like adult colouring in, and I was worried that I would feel silly or inauthentic. You don't have to proclaim it to the world, or even write it down, though. You can just do it in your head. Some days are totally shit, and there's no getting around it, but most of the time you can find something small to be grateful for; whether it's the first sip of a hot drink, or the loveliness of your child's smooth, cool cheek against yours. Reminding yourself that you have something of real value – even if you don't have Gucci loafers – can be a real game-changer.

- **Remind yourself that it simply isn't all real**
  The reason that social media makes us feel inadequate is, perhaps, partly because it gives us access to the lives of those with more money/a better career/a bigger house/ more pampas grass. But the key thing to remember is that it doesn't give us *open* access – we see what others want to share with us, with no deeper knowledge of their life or experiences. We don't see the arguments or the tantrums or, crucially, the credit card bills.

- **Ask yourself if you'd make the full trade-off**
  When comparing ourselves to others, we tend to pick and choose the aspects of our lives that we would swap out, given the choice – but life doesn't work that way. A useful tool for keeping comparison in check is to ask yourself whether, if a genie were to come along and offer to switch you with whoever you're comparing yourself unfavourably to, you would say yes. The full package – their partner, their children, their extended family, their dog. You don't get to keep anything about your own life. I find this exercise helps me to realize what it is in my life that I wouldn't give up for any amount of money,

and also reminds me of the less fantastic elements of the lives of others.

It's so easy to compare ourselves to others online – what's harder, sometimes, is to remember what's actually important and inspirational to us in the face of so many other opinions. It's been raised with me a number of times that, in jumping on every Instagram bandwagon, we risk losing our ability to think as individuals and, if we're not careful, we'll all end up with the same spotty dresses and Berber rugs. One of the huge appeals of Instagram is that it's a place where people can share their creativity and individuality, but that joy is lost if we start basing our opinions on what everyone else is sharing, and forget about our own personal taste.

You can't buy happiness via an affiliate link

Without the feelings of comparison and inadequacy addressed in my previous point, influencer marketing doesn't work nearly as well. Brands rely on the fact that not only can a specific influencer make you want something specific, but also that the more influencers a person follows, the more normalized the practice of constant consumerism becomes. In other words, the more Joneses there are to keep up with, the harder we work to keep up with them – we see somebody on an expensive holiday, somebody else posing outside Peggy Porschen, another person talking us through their latest fashion haul, and we feel we have to be doing ALL of those things too. The symbiotic relationship between influencers and brands means that popular social media accounts rely on brand partnerships both to fund them and to provide content, while brands fight to be featured by an ever-increasing pool of Insta-famous personalities in order to stay current. The right influencer can sell out a dress or event within hours.

I have seen it argued that social media influencers get a hard rap compared to celebrities, who have always been gifted designer products and paid astronomical advertising fees, and I can see the logic. But there's a crucial difference, which is that the majority of lifestyle bloggers, interiors influencers and 'Insta-mums' we follow are positioned as being 'just like us' – the reason being that most of them genuinely were, to begin with at least. We feel like we should be experiencing a comparable lifestyle because they are relatable – they get spots, they have periods and they talk about the school run and putting the bins out. They talk directly to us on Instagram stories. They sometimes DM us back. They feel like our friends.

One of the problems here is that often, as accounts grow, opportunities for partnerships with luxury brands begin to present themselves – and I can see why it would be hard to resist the opportunity to trade up. As a result of this, people who started out posting about high-street beauty and fashion – and paying for the products themselves – suddenly start advertising goods at a much higher price point, which are gifted by the brands they are working with. It's easy to see why followers, who might have once treated themselves to a couple of recommendations from their favourite lifestyle blogger every now and again, might find themselves either spending more than they can afford in order to keep up, or feeling increasingly inadequate compared to somebody they once saw as a contemporary. One recent piece of research found that posts by top influencers featured £6,700 of luxury items, with under-40s collectively spending £400m per month trying to keep up. Unsurprisingly, the study claims that 70% of millennials and generations Z-ers are accumulating debt in order to do so.[2]

When I was managing influencer marketing in my old job, we would work on a few campaigns per season, with a monthly gifting budget for anybody who approached us, as long as they were a good fit. We had a tiered system for number of followers and engagement, telling us how much we were allowed to gift based on the numbers. I loved the creative side of it, and most of the people I worked with were lovely – diligent, open to feedback and talented in their field – but, as time went on, the exchanges became more clinical and I struggled to justify the rapidly climbing fees to my manager.

The more saturated with influencer content our newsfeeds become, the more skewed our perception of a normal lifestyle gets. Somehow it doesn't seem to properly register that the desirable products we see are gifted in exchange for coverage, even when they are properly disclosed (which doesn't always happen – more on this later). Bigger influencers are able to charge thousands of pounds in cash for a post or story and need only to send a quick email or pick up the phone in order to secure a freebie. Even for those of who know that this all goes on in theory, it can be difficult to apply that knowledge to the perfectly styled images we see every time we pick up our phones, and avoid the comparison trap.

After a period where influencer marketing was more or less completely unregulated, the ASA (Advertising Standards Authority) finally published guidelines for accounts advertising on social media in September 2018. It clearly states that advertisers are required to use hashtags to inform their followers when a post has been paid for with either cash or products,[3] but it allows too much margin for error, and some people are flouting the rules. Because enforcement is far from stringent, there are very rarely consequences for the incorrect tagging of ads, or for missing off the hashtag altogether. Influencers generally use a variety of #AD, #gifted, #pressgift, #presstrip and #spon, but I have also seen #g, #kindlyg and #sp used. It's hard to keep track, even when you're in the know, of what each of these tags might mean. Is a #presstrip the same as a gifted holiday? Does #sp mean the product was gifted, or the post was paid for? Or both? It's about as clear as mud, so there's little wonder that a September 2019 study by the ASA showed that consumers find it hard to identify what is an ad and what isn't.[4] And that's before we even start to look at the placement of the tag – I've seen them shrunk down to the tiniest text on stories, or hidden right at the bottom of a paid post, even sometimes shrouded with multiple other engagement hashtags. The industry needs proper regulation – its own regulatory body, even – and fast.

The purpose of this section is not to slate every person with a large following on Instagram – I clearly fit this description myself, after all – or to delve too deeply into the ethics of influencer marketing, but simply to make you aware of some of its flaws, and some of the traps that it's easy to fall into as a consumer of both content and goods. I have a huge amount of time for a lot of creatives who use Instagram as their mouthpiece, or as a platform for their business. I have absolutely no issue with inspirational, magazine-type content, or with people charging fees for what I now recognize to be a relentless, pretty much full-time job. But I do feel that, if you are going to make a living, or even earn any money whatsoever, from advertising on social media, you should be prepared to be completely open about it with those who choose to follow you. Use of AD or #AD is an absolute minimum, but the people who are really getting it right are those who go into more detail about a collaboration when they post. They tell their audience the exact nature of the partnership, whether the product was gifted and whether or not the brand has had any creative control over the content. They choose their partnerships carefully, and with their followers in mind.

One such person is Alex Stedman, the businesswoman behind lifestyle website *The Frugality*.[5] Alex launched her blog in 2012, sharing styling tips from her experience working in the fashion industry and writing about balancing a love of clothes with paying the bills. As a result, on her feed you will find a mixture of new, old, high street and designer fashion, and her website remains the focus of her attention – it is carefully edited and updated frequently. When I was working in interiors, I got in touch with Alex about a potential collaboration on some new upholstery lines we had launched, as she was just starting the slow renovation of her new home, and it seemed like the perfect fit. After some back and forth, however, I got the message from her agent that Alex had considered our offer, but felt that the pieces (which ranged from £300 for a footstool to almost £4,000 for a chaise sofa) would be completely unaffordable for her followers, and out of line with her message. I was professionally gutted, but personally impressed.

A few months later, I found myself talking to her in a completely different context. I had read an article she'd written and shared about her relationship with money, and it was the first time I had seen someone be that transparent on Instagram. It gave me a real confidence boost in the early days of posting about my finances online. I asked her recently about her experience of being so influential on Instagram, in particular how she balances the ads with her trademark authenticity:

I've always been very picky with ads. I don't actually work with many brands. Maybe it's from my editorial background – I used to be told from the ads team on a mag which product I 'had' to include (whether I liked it or not), whereas now I can decide what is right for my business and my audience. I've always been very clear with advertisers and brands I work with that it

has to feel authentic and be a product I believe in. I always
push back if the brand are nudging me in a direction I'm not
happy with and feels too 'sales-y'. I always go with my gut,
to be honest, and it seems to work. I have had followers tell me
I've changed or become more 'polished', but I don't take it
as a negative – I've evolved and aged and my outlook has
changed, as everyone's does.

Of course, there will always be people who would prefer their social media feeds to be kept entirely ad-free, and there are influential people who don't advertise at all. For those of us who don't necessarily mind it, but need to stay vigilant so that we are not influenced into an impulse purchase, there are ways in which we can quell those feelings of jealousy or inadequacy:

- **Curate your feed**
  'Curate' must be the buzzword of the late 2010s, but it really is the correct word in this context. I think we some-times forget that we have the power to control a lot of what we see online, so my advice here would be to ditch any hate-follows, and mute or unfollow anyone whose content doesn't make you feel good. You can change it up depending on how you feel – be flexible with who you follow.

- **Be #ad aware**
  If something looks like it might possibly be an ad, it probably is. You don't have to let that spoil your enjoyment of the photography or writing, but it's best to be aware of

whether the opinions being expressed are genuine, organic recommendations, or whether they have been briefed by the brand.

- **Take all the gloss with a large pinch of salt**
  In the same way that any Instagram feed is full of all the good stuff, influencer feeds are very carefully designed to follow a certain aesthetic. There will be a real life 'behind the squares', and it probably isn't all peachy.

- **Remember that there's always a trade-off**
  It's worth remembering that the influencer scene isn't all peonies and little white pumpkins. Living your whole life online, open to criticism and sometimes outright trolling from others, having to source content to feed Instagram's voracious algorithm, can't always be easy.

It feels, at the moment, as though we are teetering on the edge of big changes to influencer marketing. Instagram is testing the removal of likes from posts, and the landscape of this increasingly saturated market seems to be changing. My hope is that things will be taken back in time a little, to a point when Instagram wasn't all about the ads, and when good content won out. But we'll see.

Advertising or behaviour control?

Another thing we have to contend with online, particularly on Facebook, Instagram and Pinterest, are paid ad campaigns run by retailers themselves. The incessant retargeting after we've dared to glance at a website – those interruptions on your newsfeed asking you if you've forgotten something, or offering you money off if you shop now – can be difficult to resist, and are often successful in dragging us back into that cycle of emotional shopping that we identified earlier. Especially if we've just noticed that a colleague is enjoying a lavish holiday, or the person who used to tease us at school has bought their first home, and it's made us feel a bit shit and vulnerable.

In his excellent book, *Ten Arguments for Deleting your Social Media Accounts Right Now*,[6] celebrated digital pioneer turned critical commentator Jaron Lanier gives insight into many of the different ways in which social media and, more specific-ally, the technology used behind the scenes, is changing our behaviour. I'd urge anybody to devour the whole thing, but his comments about the tricks used to get us interacting with advertising made me realize that there is a whole other level to the Facebook algorithm that is, quite frankly, terrifying. He refers to advertising on social media not as advertising, but as 'behaviour modification', because, he claims, that is essentially what it is. The ability of Facebook's algorithms to determine things about our online behaviour, and then to serve us content that pushes us to make certain decisions, is astonishing. Lanier writes:

> *Are you sad, lonely, scared? Happy, confident? Getting your period? Experiencing a peak of class anxiety? So-called*

advertisers can seize the moment when you are perfectly primed, and then influence you with messages that have worked on other people who share traits and situations similar to yours.

Scary, isn't it?

While Lanier's book opened my eyes to the sheer depth of behaviour control involved in Facebook advertising, I already had some insight into the lengths that advertisers will go to in order to make a sale. In a previous job, I was invited to some workshops at Facebook HQ in London, and the entire focus of one seminar was 'removing friction' from the customer journey, all the way from their first interaction with the advert to the 'thank you for your purchase' page. They advised things like optimising page loading times and creating a path to conversion (the things you have to do in order to make a purchase) that involved as few clicks as possible. Things like in-platform shopping on Facebook and Instagram – where you don't even have to leave the app to complete your purchase – and Amazon 1-Click or PayPal One Touch are designed to give you as little time as possible to actually think about what you're doing. What they call 'friction' is really just 'the time and space one needs to make an informed decision'. Adding friction is something we do for vulnerable people, such as gambling addicts, so that they can't easily fall into destructive spending behaviour, but if a loss of friction is so harmful, then why are we allowing other consumers to slip down the slope to financial difficulty?

I hope that the insights and advice in this chapter can help you to claw back some friction in this increasingly slippery online environment. I've fallen victim to the temptation that comes from being served a 20-per-cent-off code for something I'd already decided wasn't quite right, reinvigorating it with a new level of allure, too many times. I've panic bought at the merest mention of 'last few remaining' (in one instance, a shelf that I didn't even have permission from my landlord to mount on the wall), and lost precious hours scrolling through endless carousels of fast-fashion pieces. I have fallen for every trick in the book, even when I knew what was going on behind the scenes.

When I first started working in social-media marketing, Facebook advertising was a lot less sophisticated than it is now, but it could still target and retarget shoppers in an alarmingly meticulous way even then. Using all of the breadcrumbs of information that we leave behind as we cruise around the internet with not a care in the world, Facebook can single you out as a likely prospect based on a number of criteria. You might be a good bet because of a particular interest you've expressed through the pages you like, or because of a particular tendency you have – such as spending on a credit card. That's right, there is an audience in the 'behaviour' category of the Facebook advertising platform called 'credit card spenders'. And, you won't be surprised to hear, it usually performs really well.

We *can* beat the urge to click, but it means that we have to manually start adding that friction back in ourselves. There are little rules that we can set for ourselves that mean we're forced to confront the fact that we're actually spending, rather than tripping and falling into a purchase with our eyes closed. Here are a few steps I'd recommend taking, if you know this is an area where you struggle:

- **Force yourself to sleep on it**
  If you are prone to impulse purchases that you go on to regret, make a rule that you will always wait 24 hours before any purchase from paid advertising. Advertisers often use urgency – time-limited offers or low stock availability, for example – to make sales. Don't allow yourself to be rushed. I used to think of missing out on a discount, or something I wanted selling out, as a tragedy. But often, when given the space to properly consider a purchase, we find we're not really that bothered anyway.

- **Make paying more difficult**
  This could mean something as simple as removing your card details from PayPal and autofill, or even getting rid of your autosaved passwords. At the very least, ensure that credit cards or store-card accounts take more than just a couple of clicks to spend with. Yes, it means that necessary or considered purchases take more time to complete, but we have to somehow re-link the pleasure of buying with the pain of paying if we are to use consequence as a factor in our decision making, rather than leaving that mess for our future selves to clean up.

- **Remember that it's real money**
  Imagine that somebody came into the room where you are currently sitting, and dropped the cash for the thing you're about to buy into your lap. Is this really what you would spend it on? If the answer is yes, go ahead. If the answer is no, it means that you have other priorities, and you need to scroll on past.

Social media can feel like a money and mental-health minefield but, unlike Lanier, I don't think we necessarily need to delete all of our accounts or disengage entirely. What we need to do is learn to use it with greater care, and to remember that it is supposed to enhance our experience of life, not consume it. If we feel ourselves engaging in behaviour that we know isn't good for us, or losing our sense of self, we need to be able to step away. There is so much to enjoy, but there's also a lot at stake – take care of yourself out there.

Five

Finance is a Feminist Issue

At the time of writing, 97% of my Instagram followers are women, and as such, it seems only right to talk about the financial challenges that are unique to being female. We are paid less, targeted more by advertisers, and we pay a 'pink tax' on any number of different life essentials. We lose out in our careers because we're the default primary carers of our children (and sometimes parents too), we feel less confident investing, and one in five of us find personal finance more awkward to discuss than periods.[1] Even periods themselves are a massive financial burden for some, costing an average of £4,800 over the course of a lifetime.[2]

Despite a significant amount of media attention in recent years, the gender pay gap has barely shifted since 2012,[3] and there is nothing to say that it is going to get better any time soon. Because of a complete lack of transparency around salaries in most companies – in my previous place of work, it was the only thing we were strictly forbidden from disclosing to one another – it can be almost impossible to determine whether or not we are being underpaid compared to our male peers. A study by Good Money Week, a campaign that aims to grow awareness of ethical finance, showed that 27% of women had never asked for a pay rise, compared with only 18% of men, and that women were far more likely to feel awkward doing so.[4] I certainly know that feeling.

For all of these reasons and more, women are more likely to have debt – in fact, 64% of people struggling with debt in the UK are female.[5] They are also less likely to feel confident in their own judgement when it comes to money, with a study showing that a shocking 69% of millennial women in the UK defer to their male partners for long-term financial decisions.[6]

Until I started engaging with these kinds of statistics, and thinking about my own behaviour and experiences, I had never really considered that my being a woman had determined anything about my financial situation. Of course, I recognized the financial burden that having children had placed on me, and how it had disrupted my career, but the less obvious aspects of gender inequality had more or less completely escaped my notice.

I'd like to explore the reasons why women are at such a financial disadvantage, and reflect on what, if anything, we can do about it. I hope that, in identifying the unique financial challenges facing women at the moment, we can begin to combat them – both on an individual level and by engaging with campaigns that further our collective cause. It's time for an end to the hypocrisy of paying women less for equivalent work, and yet perpetuating the idea that all women – and particularly young women – are spendthrifts who waste all of their money on shoes and handbags. I'm encouraged by the recent groundswell of women writers and experts starting to address the subject of female finance, but we have a way to go before we level the playing field when it comes to cash.

Mind the gap

When it comes to earning money, there are a number of ways in which women lose out. The gender pay gap – not the same as gender pay discrimination, which is where there is a difference between what men and women working in the same job earn – is a complex calculation that uses a number of different criteria to work out how much money, on average, women miss out on over the course of their careers. Each year, the Fawcett Society determines the date of Equal Pay Day[7] – the date in the year after which the average woman in the UK is effectively working for free, compared to men. In 2019, it was 14 November, meaning that women are currently losing out on about six weeks' worth of pay. That's equal to a gap of 13.1% for full time workers, and 16.2% when part-time employees are included.[8] Because women are more likely to work part time while raising their children, the reasons for which we'll go into a little later, we are frequently losing out on opportunities and our earning potential is limited.

Women have a legal right to equal pay for equal work, but the lack of pay structure transparency in most organisations means that many women have no idea whether or not they are being paid the same as their male counterparts. According to the Fawcett Society, women are being let down by a loophole in the law that is supposed to make pay discrimination illegal in that employers do not have to disclose pay data to employees. This means that, although a woman may suspect she is being underpaid compared to men doing work of equal value, she is unable to hold her employers to account unless she can get hold of the information in another way. In many workplaces, discussing salaries is simply not allowed. Pay discrimination is a huge factor in the overall gender pay gap, and if women don't have the right to know when they're being paid less, there is little hope of us being able to close it. What really stings about this is that, where we are able to prove pay inequity, that law is on our side – as demonstrated by high profile cases such as Samira Ahmed's recent sex discrimination win against the BBC,[9] which will hopefully act as a precedent for women who are being short-changed in the workplace.

Because this is a legal and societal problem, rather than an individual one, it's difficult to see what we might be able to do to improve our own circumstances when it comes to unequal pay. All I can recommend is that you remain convinced of your right to be paid equally for equal work – that you ask for the pay rises you feel you deserve, you go for the promotions even though you work part time, and you apply for well-paid jobs – and that you never, ever question your value based on your gender.

Money and motherhood

One of the gifts of being more open about our money problems, even with friends who I know to be much better off, is that we've been able to discuss the impact of having children on even the most stable of financial situations. It makes me feel a bit better. A friend of mine, with children roughly the same age, recently declared to me that there was 'absolutely no comparison between life before and after kids' with regards to money.

She's absolutely right. For most of us, having children has a crippling double-effect on our finances. Children cost money to feed and clothe – and those Water Babies classes aren't going to pay for themselves at £16 a pop – but they also have a grave impact on our earning potential and career progression, especially if we dare to request part-time or flexible hours.

Over the course of the last year, I have received an astonishing number of messages from women who identified maternity leave as the beginning of their financial struggles, for a variety of reasons. Some weren't able to save in preparation for the drop in pay, which is a situation that I've found myself in. Some simply weren't prepared for the impact of statutory maternity pay. Some were made redundant, or weren't able to return to work for any number of reasons. Some felt pressured into spending more than they could afford on their baby, in order to feel like an adequate parent. Some developed post-natal depression or anxiety, and all of the complicated feelings and spending habits that, as we've already established, come along with mental health challenges. Of course, none of us would exchange our children for an injection of cash, but I will admit that there have been moments when I have found it difficult to silence that voice in the back of my head – the one that reminds me how much financial trauma could have been avoided if we had waited to have a second child, or just not had one at all. And even though I know how ferociously I love my youngest son, there is an avalanche of guilt that follows any thoughts remotely resembling regret about his arrival.

There is an awful lot to process and unpick regarding all this and, unlike with some of the previous factors we've discussed, much of what follows requires huge changes in attitudes and governmental policy that are out of our control as individuals. But there are movements that we can lend our voices to and, in any case, it helps to be reassured that others are also finding both their personal and financial resources stretched wafer thin, struggling to afford family life in terms of both money and time. It helps to know that it really is that hard, for most people, not just for us.

Maternity leave and working after children

According to a 2018 study, a quarter of new parents in the UK are taking on debt in order to make ends meet, relying on credit to bolster the meagre income provided by statutory parental pay.[10] At the time of writing, new and expectant mothers are entitled to six weeks at 90% of their full pay, followed by 39 weeks at either £148.68 per week or 90% of their average weekly earnings, whichever is lower. The same weekly rate applies to shared parental pay, but men taking leave are not entitled to the initial six weeks at 90%. When we consider that the median weekly salary for full-time employees in the UK is currently around £585,[11] this seems quite the adjustment to have to make. Of course, some employers offer enhanced maternity packages that entitle women to a more generous allowance, but these are, in my experience, not easy to come by, and often come with fairly stringent conditions. The poor maternity pay available to women in the UK puts a strain on family finances, but it also robs women of their financial independence at a time when they are arguably at their most vulnerable already. Women on maternity leave are completely reliant on a transparent and fair financial relationship with their partner or spouse (if they have one), which, sadly, is not always the case. For money worries to cast such a huge shadow over what should be a happy time is a massive shame, and yet it's happening to a huge number of families in the UK, as I discovered when I asked my audience to share their experiences:

> *The money side of maternity leave has been the toughest, and at times I have lain in bed with anxiety about the lack of cash and the dependence on my partner – plus the strain on our relationship and the debt it has caused. On top of that, I feel guilty for not having the most beautiful nursery, and not*

being able to afford a house with a playroom, or holidays to Disneyland. Ultimately I know these aren't important, but it's tough to be resilient to that pressure to have it all when you're so exhausted.

Being on maternity leave was one of the scariest times of my life – months of dread and confusion about how I would afford my daughter. It wasn't blissful for me, as it appeared to be for my friends – I spent each day trying to spend as little money as possible, and only managed to take 12 weeks in total. I then returned to work to find that people were judging me for leaving my daughter in full-time childcare – like I'd had a choice.

My personal experience of maternity leave and pay was that I found it unsettling not knowing exactly how much I was going to get paid each month. As is the case for many other new parents, the financial anxiety caused by such a drop in income impacted my enjoyment of my new baby. When I had my second son, we were already skating on thin ice, financially speaking. Shortly after he was born, my husband and I began to talk about the possibility of shared parental leave. Although he was the main breadwinner, he only earned slightly more than me, but was working an average of twenty hours a week more. He was burning out, and I was itching to get back to work for reasons that are entirely alien to me now. I was ambitious and keen to progress in my role, and I knew that my team were under-resourced without me there, so we agreed that, if I could negotiate a small pay rise, we would swap. The meeting went better than I could have hoped for. Effusive praise. An agreement to change my job title, increase my responsibilities and review my salary. I was thrilled. So thrilled, in fact, that I neglected to follow up in writing – a mistake that seems unforgivably stupid now, but I genuinely trusted my boss.

At no point had I been asked to keep my news under wraps, but I didn't tell anyone about the outcome of the meeting to begin with, privately enjoying the feeling that I was finally getting some recognition. Weeks went by and, shortly before I was due to return full time, I mentioned to a couple of colleagues that I was looking forward to starting my new role. Big mistake. Huge.

Later that week, I received an email from my boss downplaying almost everything that had been said in our meeting and admonishing me for my lack of discretion. I was used to a very open company culture, where nothing (apart from money) was kept under wraps, and the Managing Director would casually announce big decisions as soon as he stepped out of the meeting where they had been decided. But our MD had taken a leave of absence while I was away, and things had obviously changed. I felt utterly humiliated, and foolish to have thought that I was worthy of a promotion in the first place. I had no idea how much the company culture had changed, and was left to conjure up all kinds of scenarios in my head. I screwed my courage to the sticking place and responded with an email that belied how I felt in real life, reiterating exactly what my understanding of our meeting had been, and setting straight a few comments that had been taken wildly out of context. Things were resolved, but for me, the damage was done. The wait to go back to work was agony, but it was too late to change my mind; the wheels were in motion for my husband's leave, and there was no time to find another job.

Quite apart from the anxiety of returning to an environment that now felt completely hostile, I had the added worry of not being able to secure that vital pay rise. In the five months that followed, I chased it up three times to no avail, each occasion more awkward than the last. A token increase was finally granted just as I was interviewing for other jobs, but I knew that I needed to leave. Any successes I had – and there were a few – felt empty, and I didn't know who I could trust. I stuck to conversations about *Bake-Off* and baubles, and spent my lunch breaks on the phone to recruiters.

For all that this was an unpleasant experience, and had a negative impact on our family finances at a time when there was no room for manoeuvre, I'm not convinced there was anything discriminatory about it (beyond the fact that I was on leave, and not able to defend myself when the rumour mill started whirring). It was, by and large, a fairly good company to work for as a parent. Maternity pay was statutory, and the working day had little flexibility built in, but I was able to work one day a week from home to ease the transition for me and my four-month-old baby. If either of my children were ill,

I was able to stay at home with them, as long as I was on email or at the end of the phone. People were allowed to leave early for school plays, or to take their children to the dentist. It definitely could have been worse. For many women, returning to work from maternity leave is fraught with anxiety through absolutely no fault of their own, without them having set a foot wrong – as I unintentionally had.

Founded by maternal rights powerhouse Joeli Brearley, the Pregnant then Screwed campaign provides support to women facing all types of discrimination during pregnancy, maternity leave and when they return to work. What she refers to as 'the motherhood penalty' is clearly laid out on the homepage of their website in a series of shocking statistics:

- 54,000 women a year are pushed out of their jobs due to pregnancy or maternity leave
- 77% of working mums have encountered negative or discriminatory behaviour at work
- 33% of employers say they would avoid hiring a woman of childbearing age
- 44% of working mums say they earn less than they did before having children[12]

In her campaigning work, Joeli is frequently heckled by people who misunderstand her mission, and shares these messages, usually of the 'if you can't afford 'em, keep your legs shut' variety, on her Instagram stories. What these people don't seem to get – apart from the basic requirements of not being a total arsehole – is the fact that anything to do with maternity discrimination is not just a problem for women. It is a problem for families – which often include men, and always, for the purpose of this discussion, include children. That is the crux of this problem. It is not just making women broke, it's making families broke. It is adding an extra, incredibly stressful layer to what already feels like a manic juggle most of the time.

For the women who are pushed out of their jobs, meanwhile, it can be difficult to get back on to the career ladder – not only because of the logistical nightmare of job-hunting with a tiny baby, but because of the devastating effect that an experience like that can have on your confidence.

Childcare

Anyone who has ever been handed a nursery bill will know that the burden of childcare costs is a heavy one. When my eldest son was in nursery full-time, our monthly invoice was more than our rent, and it left us very little to live on. For a two-parent family not in receipt of benefits, childcare in the UK is more expensive than anywhere else in the world,[13] and decent subsidies do not kick in until children are three years old. This means that, for a lot of families, it is prohibitively expensive for both parents to work. Childcare costs are held up against the salary of one parent – in the vast majority of cases the mother, because they are likely to be earning less – and a decision is made about whether or not it is financially worthwhile for her to return to work. But if a woman stays at home with her child – not through choice, but through necessity – until childcare becomes more affordable after three years, how do we expect her to just pick up where she left off before maternity leave? The other option, of course, is to return to work in order to keep your career (more or less) on track, but to simply break even, or make a loss.

Not only does the monthly cost of childcare make a severe dent in all but the largest of incomes, but there are often fees to be paid upfront, and invoices are usually due a month in advance. This means that, even if parents can just about afford the monthly payments, some just can't get over the initial hump after months on a reduced income. I still get anxious around nursery invoice time. We have to pay by the end of the month, a month in advance – meaning that if we want to take advantage of the 20% top up from our tax-free child-care account, we effectively have to pay two months ahead, because payments through the portal take up to five working days to reach your provider.

Even apart from the astronomical cost, the time constraints are enough to make most of us go cross-eyed. I have been that mother skidding into the car park two minutes after nursery closes, preparing my excuses and apologies as I dash to the door, because my work hours were 8:30 a.m.–5 p.m., and my sons' nursery's opening hours were 8 a.m.–5:30 p.m., and I worked half an hour away. As well as the obvious and expected restrictions, there are also the subtle ones. You can't stay that extra five minutes to pitch an idea to your boss, or finish an email, or tidy your desk, and suddenly you're aware that you are, through no fault of your own, coming across as less committed than your colleagues. You look around the room as you slip your coat on two minutes before the end of your working day, wondering if anyone is noticing, judging. It is these small insecurities that add up, and can undermine our ability to ask for that pay rise, or to put ourselves forward for promotion. They make us doubt ourselves, make us question our dedication to our work, make us less likely to feel deserving of recognition. We are expected to parent as though we don't work, and work like we don't have children – and when we can't meet these impossible expectations, we feel we have failed everyone.

Our impossible standards as mothers, and what they cost us

As well as the devastating double-whammy of earning less and having to pay out most of that reduced salary on childcare, there are other, less overt financial strains placed on mothers. They begin the moment you find out you're pregnant, and continue through your children's childhoods, and probably for the rest of their lives. They are the things we convince ourselves are absolutely essential in order for our child to thrive, from the perfectly packed hospital bag and the extortionate sleep aids to the baby sensory classes and the after-school activities. When we are pregnant or post-natal, especially for the first time, we are unbelievably vulnerable to advertising –

and marketers know this. We are often isolated, hormonal and completely freaked out. Our confidence in our own ability to make decisions is often at an all-time low as we grapple with the massive changes to our life, and any product that promises a better night's sleep, easier feeding, less crying or more stimulation is difficult to resist. If something is supposedly good for our baby's development, we feel that we are being neglectful not to at least give it a go. We are awake and scrolling at weird times of the night, our half-asleep brains unable to make informed and sensible decisions. We feel like everyone else knows something we don't, so we jump on any recommendation with hope in our eyes and a credit card in our hand.

As I've mentioned, our first son was not planned. I'd been diagnosed with a condition that affected my fertility, leading to a slightly cavalier attitude towards contraception. *Et voilà*: a positive pregnancy test and a frantic scramble by my husband and I to throw together something approximating a normal family life. For this reason, and also because I was only twenty-five when he was born, I always felt there was extra pressure on me to prove that I could be a good mother. To give him everything he would have had if he had come along ten years later in our lives, when we were more prepared. I would compare our setup to that of the other families in our NCT group, feeling woefully inadequate, and try to keep up, booking the same activities and buying the same toys. I didn't even consider buying second-hand, as I wanted everything to be shiny and new. Baby clothes were my gateway into the realms of the Next directory store card, a debt that I have only just cleared – five years, a very uncomfortable sofa and a couple of thousand pounds later.

During my second maternity leave, I no longer felt the need to prove myself as a mother per se, but by then I had been sucked into the world of Insta-perfect motherhood. Even the people who were talking about shitty nappies and pukey hair had Instagram feeds that belied the realities of life with a young baby – endless photos of them doing a perfectly-timed yawn, clad in handmade, organic clothes. This was when my emotional spending reached a peak. It wasn't just the aesthetic that I found alluring; I think it was the thought of being part of a community. When you have a tiny baby, your identity can feel fragile and precarious, as if someone took the mould away when you weren't quite set yet, and I think that makes 'fitting in' in an environment like Instagram even more appealing. If you're not sure who you are as a person any more, it's okay, because you can be one of the mums with the Tiba & Marl changing bag and the MOTHER sweatshirt.

For working mums, 'mum guilt' can also come with a financial cost. When I asked about emotional spending on Instagram, feeling guilty about not being with our children enough came up again and again:

Being a full-time working mum makes me feel I have to make up for lack of contact with treats.

Feeling like I'm a bad mum because I'm not around as much makes me feel I need buy all the things for my daughter.

These are all certainly things I've felt myself. I'm lucky enough to still be friends with most of the women I did NCT with – for those of you who don't know about NCT classes, you basically pay for some new friends who will be dealing with colic and cracked nipples at exactly the same time as you – but when I had to return to work earlier than they did, and full time rather than part time, it resulted in a sort of cocktail of jealousy, guilt, and feeling like the odd one out. Seeing less of my son meant that I felt under enormous pressure to try to make every moment with him special, splashing out on day trips and gifts in an attempt to prove that I loved him just as much as mothers who could afford to dedicate more of their time to child-rearing. It's so difficult not to fall into that trap, because the urge to overcompensate can be incredibly strong – and that little squeal of delight when you give them a gift or announce an expensive day trip really can help to assuage the guilt, at least temporarily. With so little time, and so much to do, giving your child the time and attention that they crave while also working to pay the bills can feel impossible, but I have found that making space for a couple of short games or activities every day can make a huge difference. To most children, five minutes of your full, undivided attention is worth a *lot* of Kinder Eggs.

Self-esteem, body image and letting go of perfection

Of course, it's not just mothers who hold themselves to these impossibly high standards. Women in general are prone to such severe self-criticism that I sometimes wonder how we manage to get anything else done. We so frequently feel that our efforts are not enough, and the temptation to try to make up the difference with a purchase is often too strong to resist.

It's difficult to know how much of this is in our nature, and how much of it is how we are conditioned by the media and society. Women are taught from a very young age that there are things that we absolutely *must* do and be in order to be accepted. We must be beautiful, slim and body hair-free to be of value, for example. Then, we are sold products to help us to achieve this – weight-loss aids, waxing kits, hair products, make up. A cynic might say that we are instilled with this insecurity precisely so that we can be marketed to more successfully.

When is it, I wonder, that the burning desire to fix ourselves at any cost starts to kick in? Is it puberty? Earlier? I can't say for myself when I started to notice that other girls' legs were longer and slimmer, their faces more delicate, the hair on their arms finer, less visible. I don't remember the first time I looked in the mirror and hated what I saw. I don't remember the first time I declared myself 'on a diet'.

My distorted relationship with food and my appearance has ebbed and flowed over the years, finally settling into something roughly resembling a truce after I had my eldest son. Something about having grown and birthed a child seemed to soothe my desire for the perfect body, and my broken metabolism seemed to repair itself a little. But during that decade that I spent unable to look in the mirror without composing my face and sucking in my stomach, the amount I spent on seeking solutions doesn't bear thinking about. The magic thigh-shrinking seaweed wraps that I ordered online, forgetting to cancel the subscription that ended up costing me almost half of my student-maintenance loan. The gym memberships I would use either obsessively or not at all. The diet books, the workout DVDs, the protein shakes, the zero-calorie noodles, the dumbbells, the green-tea capsules. The endless, endless clothes for a body that I was not made to have. The wardrobe designed for a better me, a me that could just stick to the fucking diet, for God's sake. It was toxic, and it perpetuated my struggle to accept my body or maintain a healthy weight, because I was stuck in a cycle of deprivation and over-indulgence. Sound familiar?

It took me a long time to make the connection between how I felt about the way I looked and how I spent my money, and even longer to realize that this isn't all that uncommon. It hadn't even occurred to me to include this aspect of my mental-health history in this book, until I asked about emotional spending triggers in one of my Q&A sessions, and about a fifth of responses were related to low self-esteem, citing feeling 'fat', 'ugly' or 'insecure' as catalysts for buying unneeded and sometimes even unwanted items. I found myself nodding along with the descriptions of the ways in which people tried to fix – buying trendy, overpriced 'superfoods', for example – or distract from – buying clothes for their baby because they resented their post-natal shape – these insecurities. For me, certainly, the need to look 'better' transcended any importance I placed on healthy finances.

I don't feel that way about my body any more, most of the time. I can tolerate the stretchmarks on my stomach and the hint of a double chin (which remained even when I was at my very thinnest) with a level of neutrality I wouldn't have thought possible for most of my twenties. But the pursuit of perfection isn't so easily abandoned, and clearly my obsession with fixing my appearance was replaced with other, equally unhealthy fixations.

When our poor relationship with money and erratic spending habits come from a place of low self-worth and a desire to fix what we perceive to be wrong with us, it can be difficult to see a way out. If we can safely assume that we're not all about to fall off a treadmill and suffer a confidence-boosting head injury à la Amy Schumer in I Feel Pretty, then perhaps the answer lies in a gentler form of self-acceptance. I've always been fascinated by the body positivity movement, but at times I find it almost as intimidating as the perfect bodies that used to taunt me from the pages of magazines. For a long time, the prospect of loving my body, of accepting that it didn't need to be fixed, seemed as far-fetched as magically waking up as Gigi Hadid one morning. But over the last year or so, the body neutrality movement has been creeping higher in my awareness, and I've found something refreshing – astonishingly so, really – in the idea that you can be happy and successful regardless of how you look. That the size and shape of your body have no bearing on how worthy you are. I suppose that what we are aiming for – what I hope to give you, with this book – is a sort of money neutrality in the same vein. The ability to separate your finances from your sense of self-worth, and live your life free of the grip of perfectionism and money shame.

As women, we face a unique challenge when it comes to finance. Not only are we engaged in a battle to level the playing field when it comes to progressing in our careers and earning money, but we are also faced with a barrage of messages about how we should be spending it too. Capitalism thrives on our discontentment with the way that we look – the global weight-loss industry is projected to be worth almost $245billion by 2022[14] – and most of these products are targeted heavily towards women. We are told we're not good enough, and then flogged solutions for the problems we've been tricked into believing we have. We need to tackle both of these things, at once – and we will. Watch out, patriarchy.

A note from Joeli Brearley

It was when I was facing my own difficult time at work that I found Joeli and her campaign, Pregnant then Screwed. Joeli's knowledge and passion in the area of work and motherhood are second to none.

The labour market doesn't work for mothers. It was set up by men at a time when women did their work in the home, unpaid. That set up doesn't work any more because the cost of living is so much higher, so most mothers need to work, many also want to. Pregnancy and maternity discrimination affects 77% of working mums, but that isn't the only barrier. Lack of high-quality flexible jobs and astronomical childcare costs both contribute to what we call 'the motherhood penalty'. While dads get pay rises and promotions, mums get demoted, sacked, made redundant and have their income drastically reduced. The Institute of Fiscal Studies says that by the time a woman's first child is twelve years old, her hourly pay rate is 33% behind a man's. Clearly, this enormous disparity between the earnings of mothers and fathers affects women throughout their life and results in far too many elderly women living in poverty.

Throughout our lives both men and women work very hard, it's just that one gets paid handsomely for the work they do, and the other doesn't. It's time for change. It's time for equality.

Six

'Oh, You're Still Renting?'

We don't own our home. It is a subject that I have skirted around with colleagues and acquaintances for a long time. I've pretended to friends that we were somewhere on the way to having a deposit together, even when we were in the thickest fog of financial difficulty, limping through to the end of each month. I've spent hours scrolling though properties on Rightmove. I've opened a Lifetime ISA and optimistically put a couple of hundred quid into it. I've been in denial about how difficult it is to get on to the property ladder, if you haven't been gifted a deposit, been able to live with your parents while you save, or started working towards home ownership as soon as you entered full-time employment. Those millennials with the opportunity to earn a good wage, and the foresight to make buying a house a priority right from day one of their careers, may have just about scraped a deposit together on their own, but for anybody whose life has taken a different route, the prospect of getting out of rented accommodation is getting more and more unrealistic.

In the wider context of money and debt, owning property usually works in your favour. Better rates are often available to those who own rather than rent, and your accommodation status is always taken into account in credit applications. There is also, of course, the fact that downsizing or remortgaging are often possible for anyone with equity who is looking for a long-term solution to their debt, which puts them at an advantage over those without bricks-and-mortar assets. It's not the ultimate solution, and there are many reasons why owning a home might be more of an albatross than an asset, but it can make a difference.

For me, home ownership isn't just about status and possession, it's about emotions. It's about the feeling of security that you get from knowing that your landlord can't turf you out with two months' notice for whatever reason they choose, of feeling that you are building something, putting down some roots. Despite the fact that a fifth of the UK population are now living in privately rented accommodation – a figure which has doubled in the last twenty years and is set to increase to a quarter by 2021[1] – attitudes to renters in the UK are still fairly appalling, especially outside of London. We don't feel trusted and respected because, by and large, we aren't.

Most of us aren't trusted to keep a pet or decorate according to our own taste, for example, both of which are ways that we, as adults, might build a 'home'. It feels like life is put on hold, but with a study by the Resolution Foundation suggesting that half of millennials will rent until their forties, with a third never owning a home in their lives, where does that leave us?

According to journalist and housing rights campaigner Vicky Spratt, it presents us with a problem not only now, but also for generations to come. I have deferred to Vicky's expertise on this subject throughout this chapter, after a wonderful interview that helped me to decipher some of my own complicated feelings about my status as a renter, and to understand the socio-economic factors at play.

It should be noted that, if you rent in the UK and are thinking of moving soon, you have Vicky to thank for the fact that you no longer have to pay extortionate agent admin. fees, or more than five weeks' worth of rent for your deposit. Her 2016 Make Renting Fair campaign, which highlighted the difficulties faced by 'Generation Rent', succeeded in getting letting fees abolished, effective from June 2019. As someone who is likely to rent for at least another few years, I'd actually like to take this opportunity to thank her myself.

Why are we so obsessed with owning a house?

For a very long time, I laboured under what I knew, deep down, to be a complete misapprehension: that once you've got a foot on the property ladder, you're 'sorted'. That everything else falls magically into place, and you can consider yourself financially free. But the allure of home ownership, the idea of having something solid to build the foundations of a family life on, held such huge appeal for me that I allowed myself to forget that it's entirely possible to own a property and still be financially vulnerable.

The thing is that, according to statistics, the average age to buy your first home in the UK is thirty-three – so why do I, at age thirty, feel so silly for not owning property? For a while, I thought it was just because I wanted to be able to paint my home in a symphony of Farrow & Ball neutrals and drill holes wherever I wanted, but my conversation with Vicky helped me to understand just how deeply ingrained into our national mindset this obsession with home ownership really is. Clue: it's nothing to do with comparing Cornforth White and Purbeck Stone.

I think that the UK is a really interesting country in terms of how we think about housing. Up until relatively recently, most people did not own their own home. We have this whole, 'an Englishman's home is his castle' mentality and we're all desperate to get on the property ladder, but the truth is that, at the turn of the last century, most people rented, most people did not own. We went through this incredible transformation in the middle of the last century, and after World War II we had a huge drive of building social housing. We came up with this idea of a property-owning democracy, and Thatcher and everyone who came after her endorsed that view, so we became obsessed with home ownership. We're still obsessed, and I think it's now become a status symbol. Obviously, it was always aspirational, but the idea that you really haven't made it and that you're not an adult until you own your home, I think, came from that political shift. It was an incredible piece of policy that really got into the brains of people.

Much of this potted history of our housing landscape was completely new to me, but it makes perfect sense. For previous generations, buying a house became a key milestone, like graduating from university, earning your first month's salary or getting married. Those tick boxes have carried through into later generations, even though the political and economic scene has changed beyond recognition. A combination of wage stagnation and an unprecedented hike in house prices has left home ownership out of reach for many, but the need to strive for it has prevailed nonetheless.

This is made even more profound, Vicky says, because the private rented sector is not fit for purpose:

> It makes total sense that people feel this way, of course, because we do not have a private rented sector that works. What happened at the same time as Right to Buy, or around the same time, was the introduction of new regulations in the private rented sector. Up until the 1970s, we had rent control, and that was done away with by Thatcher's government. What that did was make it a lot easier for landlords to operate than for tenants to survive, and now we have this issue where our private rented sector is not fit for purpose. It's unstable and unaffordable. So, home ownership is even more appealing, because why would you rent when you could be evicted at any time, or your rent could go up at any time? It has meant that the desperation for home ownership is even more powerful than it ever was. Completely understandable, but the real kicker is that as renting becomes

*unaffordable in different parts of the country, so does home
ownership – so it's a double bind, and many people are now
caught between a financial rock and a hard place.*

I can attest to the high cost of renting, and the strain that
letting-agent fees have put on our finances time and time again.
We've had to borrow money from family in order to cover
several hundred pounds' worth of admin. fees and referencing
fees, in addition to high deposits that need to be paid out far in
advance of finding out whether you'll be getting the deposit on
your previous home back. Vicky's motivation for her campaigning was fuelled, in part, by the financial difficulties that
renting had left her in during her twenties – she accrued £11k
of debt herself while navigating the London rental market.
Where there is fierce competition for lettings, potential tenants
are often encouraged to pay holding deposits the moment they
view the property, in order to 'lock it down'. When agent fees
were legal, a transferral of these would be required to 'take the
property off the market', meaning shelling out a huge sum of
money at very short notice.

If it sounds depressing and complicated, that's probably
because it is. What it does offer, though, is some reassurance
that those of us who are staring wistfully at 'for sale' signs and
blaming ourselves for the position we find ourselves in are not
the exception. Increasingly, we are the rule. No matter how
much it feels like every single one of our peers has jumped on
to the property ladder, this is a generational problem, and it's
not all our fault. Try to take comfort from that.

The missing milestone

There seems to be an assumption that renting your home represents a state of limbo, where you mustn't get too comfortable, or think of your rented house as your home. Once, on a playdate, the parent of a friend of my son's told me that, when they were renting (while they found a suitable period property to renovate), they didn't even buy a table and chairs – they just used the patio furniture. Of course, this was a light-hearted comment that was in no way intended to wound, but as I sat in her perfect kitchen, with its tasteful extension and gleaming copper pans, I felt something inside me deflate. I have often felt uncomfortable in situations where other people are discussing mortgages and loft conversions, because I hate having nothing to contribute. It makes me feel as though I have somehow missed a crucial step in growing up, like I've missed a vital unlock on a video game and now have to go all the way back to the beginning and defeat the right boss before I can move on to the next level.

I don't think I'm alone in feeling this way. Our home ownership status is intertwined with any other money shame we have, and it's holding us back. So many of us feel too old, too bright, too married or too grown-up in other ways to still be beholden to the whim of a landlord, and we berate ourselves, often unfairly, for not having a foot on the ladder. As Carrie Bradshaw would say, we need to stop 'should-ing' all over ourselves. The rhetoric in the media about how too many lattes and avocados has scuppered our plans for home ownership falls apart under the tiniest amount of scrutiny. House prices have skyrocketed in the last twenty years, in part thanks to a booming buy-to-let market. So, to put that in real terms – people are buying houses specifically to let them out for a profit, meaning that there are fewer houses on the property market, meaning that house prices go up, meaning that more of us are trapped in private rentals. But, sure, it's the avocados.

The most frustrating thing is, it's not the monthly mortgage payments that are unaffordable to us. We pay just over £1,000 per month for a three-bedroomed terraced house in Bath, which is more than my friend's mortgage on a much bigger house. Our rent is actually on the cheap side for where we live, but it still makes up a huge proportion of our joint income and it's difficult to see, even without our debt repayments and childcare fees, how we could create enough space in our budget to save the £40k we would need for a deposit. Any time I raise the subject of renting and home-ownership on Instagram, I hear similar stories of struggling to save, eye-watering rent and huge frustration:

> *Saving for a house is all-consuming. It feels like a mountain that I'll never reach the top of, and makes saving for anything else whilst renting seem futile.*

> *My friends pay less for the mortgage on their entire flat than I do in rent for one bedroom.*

I feel like I'm constantly playing catch-up. By the time I've managed to save a bit, house prices increase and I need more for my deposit.

I recently watched an episode of *Have I Got News for You* where Ian Hislop joked – or as close as he ever gets – that millennials should be supportive of Brexit, because it was the only way they were going to be able to afford to buy a house. Even as a staunch Remainer, I did wonder if this might be one of the only benefits of crashing out – but then I reminded myself that we might lose our income, have to pay for medical care and be faced with paying £8.99 for a loaf of bread, and decided that I'd probably still rather we stayed put.

As well as how it makes us feel in terms of our progress and achievements, Vicky worries that there is an even more serious consequence for society in general, as a result of the millions of people missing this step:

When you're renting, you're not accruing any equity. You're not putting any money against your name – it's effectively going into a black hole. Of course, in return you get a roof over your head, but the quality of that roof is determined by how decent your landlord is. We need to urgently look at solutions for people who can't get deposits together because houses are so expensive now – let's face it, who can unless they use a scheme like shared ownership or Help to Buy? I don't want to be too doom and gloom about it, but the bigger picture here is that we're facing an adult social-care crisis. My grandfather was in a care home at the end of his life, and fortunately he was so unwell that he qualified for state support, but if he hadn't then the cost of that would have been looked at against the value of his house in order to fund his care. For a generation who aren't going to have any assets to sell off to pay for adult social care, what happens then? There's going to be a black hole in our public finances.

This is some serious food for thought. It means that my assumption that the housing crisis was only a problem for those of us who are unable to afford deposits is short sighted, and that this goes far beyond an individual level. The housing crisis needs to be solved, but we can't take the responsibility for that on to ourselves alone – the reality is that this should not be an issue of personal shame or inferiority; there simply is not enough affordable housing available, and many of us are stuck in private rented accommodation that devours income and leaves us unable to save.

Peaceful enjoyment and personal taste: how can we make renting better?

To avoid being too disheartened, maybe we can take a break from looking at our long-term prospects and start to think about what we can do to improve the situation on the ground. In spite of the fact that I do aspire to own a house, and I do often feel down about renting, I can appreciate that there are some benefits to being a tenant. If our circumstances were to dramatically change, or we needed to relocate, moving would be fairly quick and straightforward. When our boiler needed replacing, we weren't the ones who had to shell out for a new one. Plus, if the housing market does go south after Brexit, we won't have any capital at risk.

We are fortunate too, that we seem to have reasonable landlords, and our agency is fairly responsive – any issues we have had have usually been resolved relatively quickly, and without a fuss. Our house is warm, comfortable and largely functional.

It took us a while to make it feel like a home, however, as it had sat empty for a while before we moved in, and the bare, uneven floorboards on the ground floor needed covering. We'd shelled out a lot in letting fees and deposits, so we tried to cut costs by hiring a van and moving everything ourselves. But our house move coincided with the 'Beast from the East' of February–March 2017, and the process drained me of every bit of enthusiasm for making the place our own. We quickly discovered that there was no hot water, but our letting agent's offices were closed due to the bad weather and, in any case, no plumber would have been able to get out to us through the ice and snow. I had a minor strop – I was five-months pregnant, very tired and very sweaty, and I just wanted a bath – and went on a bit of a sweary rant about how these things should be checked before tenants move in. I was emotional and hormonal, but I'm pretty sure I was right.

Holding our agencies and landlords to account regarding things like this, and giving feedback where we have it, is one way in which we can begin to make things better on an individual level. I think that we often feel too embarrassed to report problems, or to ask for permission to make changes, because we somehow don't feel entitled to live in a comfortable environment that reflects our taste or has personal touches. But we have to remind ourselves that we're not squatting. These are our homes. They should look and feel like us from the moment you step in the front door, no matter whose name is on the deeds.

I've loved interior design for a long time. I'm fascinated by the way that stepping into a perfectly designed room can immediately lift your spirits, and the way that some people are able to create an environment that hangs together absolutely perfectly. Unfortunately for me, the scope for tenants to do much of this in their homes is limited, and renters are woefully under-represented in any content to do with interior design. In the past, if I've expressed an interest in decorating our house, or putting down carpet to minimize the draught, I've usually been met with a sort of puzzled look from my home-owning friends.

'But . . . you're renting. Isn't that a waste of money? Are you even allowed?'

Questions like this sting, but I can see the logic, sort of. It might seem silly to want to change the décor, or contribute something to the look, feel or functionality of a home that you don't own, at your own expense. Even those of us who are likely to be renting for years to come still see it as a sort of temporary state, probably because most tenancy agreements are for six or twelve months, with no guarantee of being allowed to stay for as long as you choose to. So it's little wonder that the logic of forking out for modifications when, in theory, you could be asked to move out with two months' notice at any given time, is called into question. But who wants to live in a sterile box, or put up with a poppy-red feature wall for some of the best years of their life? If you stay in one rented home for, say, five years, who is to say that you wouldn't have decorated and then redecorated within that timeframe if you owned the place?

Someone who is asking these questions, challenging perceptions of renting and fighting for a space for tenants in the world of home design, is interior stylist, author and Instagram sensation Medina Grillo. Her book, *Home Sweet Rented Home*,[2] encourages renters to unleash their creativity and make their home their own, with varying degrees of modification to suit varying degrees of landlord leniency – and different budgets. Posting as *@grillodesigns* on Instagram, she shares projects from her own rented home, and her excellent *How I Rent* video series explores the homes of tenants who have injected their own style and personality into their interiors. In addition to the aesthetic delights of her Instagram feed, Medina's captions often give voice to her insights on living in rented accommodation, and aim to destigmatize renting in a way that we don't often see in the interiors world. While mainstream publications and homeware-brand blogs run features on how to furnish your second home (eye roll), Medina is providing renters who happen to love interior design with real, affordable and landlord-friendly solutions to what has often seemed to me like an impossible problem.

My hope is that, for those of us who face a long wait until we can buy a house, there is a shift in both attitudes and policy around renting in the near future. With the rising number of private-sector renters, I fail to see how the mainstream snobbery around home ownership and the unstable terms for tenants can continue much longer. Realizing that the system is broken, that it's not just a lack of diligence or financial smarts that have left us in this situation, is helpful, I think. Despite the twinges of frustration and jealousy that still gnaw at me from time to time, I have made my peace with it – for now.

Part Two:
Taking Control

I hope that the first part of this book has helped to give you some insight into how you got here and why it's not all your fault. Now it's time to think about fixing things. Over the course of the last 150 pages or so, we've rooted out the sources of our money issues, addressed some big topics and, hopefully, started to make some progress with how we frame our financial situation in the context of our real, everyday lives.

But this is a holistic guide, not a homeopathic one. As vital as that discovery and understanding is to our progress here, those steps towards financial wellness aren't going to happen by osmosis – now that we recognize that control is within our grasp, we need to seize it, and take action.

A complicated or unhealthy relationship with money can manifest itself in a plethora of different ways – debt, difficulty saving, over-spending, feeling anxious, and much more. The advice in this second part should help you to resolve your financial demons, whatever they may be, but, most importantly, it will help you to feel in control.

The chapters that follow cover everything from getting to grips with the basics of budgeting to paying off debt and saving: whether you are battling big debt or just wondering where all of your money goes each month, there is something here for you.

I'd also like to reiterate, in case it's not clear from the first part of this book, that I'm not a financial expert. Rather than coming from years of fiscal study, this advice is based on my experience of having lived through this process – from the awkward conversations and difficult decisions to the slow progress and the genuine thrill of finally feeling in control. It also includes things I've learned from conversations with hundreds of people in similar situations – each of them leaving me more convinced that there is a gap between the expert financial opinions we are exposed to and the advice we really need.

Seven
Into the Black

This chapter is mainly aimed at people who are experiencing debt or other financial difficulties that need confronting – if this isn't you, you might want to skip straight to chapter eight, where we'll talk goals, budgeting and more.

Before you sit down with a pen, paper, calculator and perhaps a large glass of wine, it's worth noting that this is a decision to change your habits, not your whole personality. There may be elements of your character that you need to address to get there – in fact, it's pretty much essential to this process, in my experience – but you don't have to transform yourself into a #girlboss, financial expert or minimalist, if that's not who you are. I don't buy into the theory that there's a Martin Lewis inside all of us, just waiting for us to get our shit together so that he can run free. It's so tempting, when we first start to tackle any problem that's had a less than gentle grasp on our life, to feel compelled to try to wipe the slate completely clean and become a shiny new person. One who always asks for the bill to be split by item when dining with friends and takes a packed lunch to work every day without fail, who plans and batch cooks every meal, and never accidentally goes over budget on a single thing. I'm not knocking these as habits to get into – I'm just saying that it really isn't that simple if you're used to grabbing Pret sandwiches and ordering takeaways. There is no way to simply get rid of all of our emotional money baggage and start afresh; that wallet bursting with receipts for overpriced diffusers and jade facial rollers will always be with you, in your head, until you learn to let it go. The only way to lasting peace of mind is to shift our mindset, look at our actions and decide what needs to give, in order to get rid of the financial albatross that's weighing so heavily around our necks.

Now, you'll have to forgive the number of dieting analogies I'll be using over the next few chapters; they are just too perfect to resist. Despite the fact that it's still a popular model in so many areas, from food to frugality, deprivation categorically does not work for most people. It's unsustainable, and it's down-right miserable. It is self-harm. During my late teens I spent enough time living off Diet Coke and Marlboro Lights in an effort to be thin to know that deprivation and joy cannot coexist, even while you're getting the right result. It doesn't matter that you're shedding pounds per week from your waist-line or zeros off your debt, nothing ever feels good enough, because nothing is ever enough to justify what you're putting yourself through. And then, of course, you fail to meet your own impossible targets one day, usually 'derailed' by doing something that's actually enjoyable, and all of a sudden you find yourself knee deep in either Krispy Kremes or Asos orders, because what's the point in trying, anyway?

What we're looking for is a real, true mindset change, one that allows us to still be the fallible, imperfect human beings that we are, but sets us on the right path and leaves breadcrumbs for when we lose our way.

In pursuit of the lesser-spotted mindset change

I did an interview on the radio last summer, after debt expert Dr Johnna Montgomerie put forward an argument for household debt forgiveness. I'd been thinking about my position on the matter for a while, but, after a bit of soul-searching, I realized that having my debt simply written off probably wouldn't have worked for me. I realized that, had all of my debt been forgiven in January, I'd have probably already been a few grand deep on a credit card by July.

The truth is that I needed to change my mindset. I needed to do the work, to look at what mattered to me and address my spending habits. I needed to look after my mental health, and to recognize the relationship between how anxious or depressed I felt and how often I flexed my Amex. I've also found the process of paying off my debt healing. I've had to confront myself and while, yes, it's painful to see the scars of those frivolous purchases on your bank statement and credit score, it's not realistic to imagine that my behaviour would have changed without my having to completely overhaul my relationship with money.

So, we have to break the cycle and create a positive feedback system, where we can celebrate our successes in improving our finances without gleaning our entire worth from them. Annoyingly, I can't really pinpoint what exactly it was that sandblasted the scales from my eyes, but I do know that I was just really, really tired. Tired of stringing out the second fortnight of the month, paying for essentials with a rotation of credit cards. Tired of text messages from my bank warning me that it couldn't make the payments I'd arranged, and difficult phone calls that left me feeling ashamed and inept. Tired of pretending everything was fine to my friends, family and the handful of Instagram followers on my personal account, to whom I was showing only carefully styled 'shelfies' and snake-print loafers. Tired of comparing myself, my life, my children's lives, to strangers on the internet. I had reached a point where the dam of excuses and promises I'd made to myself was starting to leak, copiously, and I had to choose whether to open the release valve or watch as it groaned and splintered under the weight of all of my financial mistakes. Knowing that it was going to break very soon but not quite when, or what the damage would be. I realized that I didn't want to spend the rest of my life feeling this way. I could still, just about, see a way out, but the light at the end of the tunnel felt like it was growing dimmer, and I knew I had to decide whether to head towards it or turn my back and carry on deeper into the cave.

My husband and I were just about to start slightly better-paid jobs, and I was hopeful, for the first time in a while, that there was still a chance for us to do this ourselves. Not because there is anything at all wrong with seeking help from people equipped and trained to do so – we'll talk about this later – but because, at that time, I was still too proud to entertain the idea, and too embarrassed to admit that I needed assistance.

It's worth noting at this point that the requisite mindset change doesn't often come quickly, or easily. The decision to turn things around can be made in an instant, and I think for most people it is, but the change needed to maintain that shift is slower, and it's a constant process. When I first spewed out my money problems on to the internet, it was not necessarily with positive, long-lasting change in mind. I was angry – so, so bloody angry – with myself, mostly. Some of the motivation behind setting up the account was definitely punitive, and when I read back what I wrote in those early days, including the piece for Clemmie Telford's *Mother of all Lists*,[1] I can feel the hot fury, see it being channelled inward. As my account grew, I recognized a need to try to change the way I spoke about myself in order not to make other people in the same situation feel as though I was tearing into them as I tore into myself, and that slowly started to change the way I felt. As with any process, there were stages I had to go through before reaching the acceptance I now feel most of the time.

It's okay to be angry with yourself. It's okay to feel guilty. Skirting over those feelings, pushing them down and trying to pretend they don't exist, is a recipe for disaster later on. Face them. Examine them. Figure out what you can do about them.

As we established earlier, when you feel guilty about something, there is usually something you can do to assuage it, even just a little bit. Remember that you are not the first person to make those mistakes, and you won't be the last. Try to look at them in the context of your wider life – we have a tendency to examine our every failure under a microscope, while forgetting about the children we have managed to keep alive, the friends we've supported, or the times we've given someone a parking ticket with a couple of hours left on it. Remember that being 'bad' with money doesn't make you a bad person. Make it your mantra.

Everything we covered in part one of this book, from looking at our backgrounds and societal factors to examining our self-esteem, mental health and the way we use social media has been gearing up to this change in mindset. Give yourself the time you need to use it.

Note: You are* not going to win the lottery

*probably

I'm sorry to be the bearer of bad news.

And even if you do win, unless you put in this groundwork and fix the underlying problem, there's no amount of money that will grant you eternal financial freedom. There's a line from *Pride and Prejudice* (you'll recall that earlier on in this book I described myself as a complete fantasist? I challenge you to find me the fantasist who doesn't live at least part of their time in an Austen novel . . .) that I always though was utter bullshit growing up. Mr Bennet, having successfully married off three of his daughters during the course of the novel, laments of Jane and Mr Bingley that they will always be poor, as they are far too generous and will always live beyond their bountiful means. I think I see his point now.

Rather embarrassingly, I'd say that there was a time when winning the lottery wasn't even a back-up plan. It was more or less plan A.

I have had so many fully fleshed-out lottery fantasies that I could probably have written a book just about those. And what a lovely book it would have been. Every time I bought a ticket, I would daydream about what I was going to do with the money, fully convinced that the fact that my lucky dip numbers featured two of the digits from my birthday meant that I was destined to win the jackpot. Paying off the debt was, of course, part of the fantasy, but it was sort of skimmed over as a very small and insignificant portion of my winnings, a minor inconvenience on my way to the rolling pastures of Loaf sofas and Toast jumpers. It wasn't all selfish and super-indulgent, though: I'd imagine the joy and relief on my husband's face as I showed him the numbers, how he'd finally be able to ditch the brutal hours and we'd finally be able to have weekends as a family. I'd imagine what we could do to help out our families, who we'd do what for. But I would also imagine waltzing into the city's poshest estate agents and casually mention that we were looking to buy a property with cash, because, 'we'd been very fortunate and come into some money'.

The vividness with which I was able to conjure up these scenes is an indication of how loose my grip on the reality of our situation was during that time. The feverish imaginings would take the edge off, keep the hope alive that I was about to catapult from financial turmoil into unending decadence, but a cauldron of anxiety was bubbling away underneath, waiting to tip over.

I'd be lying if I said I hadn't also had similar fantasies of Rowling-esque success with this book, where I would sheepishly say 'Oh, I think they're about to start printing editions with "One Million Copies Sold" on the front cover', when asked the exact number by Oprah. A girl is allowed to dream. But the difference really is that I now actually have a plan for financial security, even in the event that only my mum buys a copy.

Facing the Music

What a horrible expression. For me, it conjures up those times in childhood where I, a chronic goody-two-shoes, would have to read anger or disappointment in my mum/dad/teacher's eyes. The feeling that everything was ruined, for ever. As we've already established, I am a natural ostrich, so if anything fills me with dread beyond all else, it's the concept of having to face my mistakes head on.

It is, unfortunately, a necessary step in making things okay again, but you don't have to rip your head out of the sand with such force that you burn half your face off. I know all too well those hot, anxious seconds as your internet-banking app loads, or as you open that letter you've been hiding in a drawer for months, or as you pick up the phone to your credit card company. There's only so much of that feeling that most people can cope with in a single day, and it may be that you need a gentler approach. Whether you have debt or are simply looking to make some big changes in the way you manage your money, arming yourself with all the information – the good (ha!), the bad and the ugly – is crucial, but you're allowed to give yourself the time and space you need to process it. A plaster-ripping approach works for some people, but for others, me included, an overload of bad news only serves to send us looking for the nearest emotional bucket and spade.

For those in significant financial difficulty, some experts advise sitting with a person you trust for this part of the process, in case you're in need of moral support, and if you have a go-to friend or relative who you feel could be a calm, non-judge-mental presence, then this could be really helpful.

I did it alone. I think I felt I needed the time and space to come to terms with it before reading anyone else's reaction, and that I'd struggle to find someone who would be able to be entirely neutral in that particular situation. I was also still feeling deeply ashamed, and not really ready to open up – hopefully you are making inroads in letting go of those feelings by this point, but you may still decide to do the sums by yourself.

I'd recommend taking the following steps, in the following order, and, importantly, taking a break if it all feels like it's getting a bit too much.

Note: if you can, choose a day when you're not already feeling harassed, when any kids you might have are in nursery or being looked after by someone else – and, for God's sake, don't do it when you're premenstrual. If this alignment of stars is too rare and you're booked up with annoyances for the next ten years, just pick a day when you're not already right at the end of your tether. It makes a difference, I promise. Of course, the sooner you can work out the lay of the land, the sooner you can start looking at solutions, but it's so important to protect your mental health throughout what can be a very painful and upsetting experience, at least to begin with.

---

1. Check the balance of your main account(s).
2. Check the balance of your credit card(s).
3. Download an app where you can see all your accounts in

one place, like Money Dashboard.[2]

4. Speak to someone. This could either be someone close to you, or a trained professional from a dedicated organisation – you can find a list at the back of the book. It may be that you need someone with you throughout, or you might feel you need to do this alone – it's up to you.
5. Speak to your bank and lenders.
6. Check your credit scores with all three providers.
7. Have a cup of tea (or something stronger).
8. Remember that you are more than equal to this. You are not a bad person. This is fixable. You have all the information now, and it can't hurt you any more. No more panicking because you accidentally pressed 'cash and screen balance'. No more hoping for the best when you hand over your credit card in Zara. This can be the end of all of those anxieties – right here, right now.

Opening up to friends and family

Even if you've chosen to weather the initial storm with someone who cares about you, the chances are that there are other people in your life who've been part of the audience for your Oscar-worthy performance in the latest production of *Everything is Absolutely FINE*. So, the likelihood is that there are some more awkward conversations to be had, and this can be one of the toughest parts of the whole process.

Now seems like a good time to point out that you absolutely don't *have* to tell most people – and you certainly don't have to tell them everything. I sort of did have to, because I wrote a book about it. (I still didn't tell some people exact amounts etc . . . surprise, guys!) But, in the spirit of trampling the taboo around money and debt down to a fine dust, a little opening up about how you financed your kitchen/new car/seven terms of Water Babies might actually serve to help someone else feeling the same way.

I'm not suggesting that you hotfoot it down to your local tattoo artist and get 'DEBTOR' tattooed across your forehead, or that you ask for your credit card balance to be included in the office newsletter, but financial difficulty really is a problem that can be eased by talking about it, especially with the right people. There is also the fact that changing your relationship with money and getting on the right track towards financial freedom is going to mean some lifestyle changes, which may or may not be noticeable to others, depending on how extreme the changes are and how closely people are paying attention. One of the most common questions I get asked is 'How do I tell x that I can't afford to do y?'

If you asked that question in the lawless wastelands of the Mumsnet opinion threads, you would no doubt be told that 'No is a complete sentence' – in other words, you don't owe anyone an explanation. While that's nice in theory, I'm not sure how well it will go down in reality when you are trying to explain why you're not doing Christmas presents this year, or why you can't fly to St Bart's for cousin Sebastian's destination wedding. If you've always lived by a principle of saying no to as few people as possible in order to avoid letting anybody down, these new boundaries might be hard to put into place at first, and that's where opening up a little about the realities of your finances can prove helpful.

Talking to your partner

There's a reason that this one is first. It may be that your partner is completely up to speed with your finances, in which case the main thing you need to agree on is how you are going to tackle things, but hidden debt is a surprisingly common issue in relationships.

If you have a partner, and you share money and responsibilities, there is no getting around the fact that they have a right to know about any debt or struggles. For a long time, I didn't do a very good job of this. I managed our family finances and made a lot of the decisions that lead to our debt, and although it wasn't a secret, it wasn't something we spoke openly about. We both knew things weren't going well, but we only ever addressed it when there was an immediate threat, and we were too set in our habits for those brief moments of panic to be catalysts for change in themselves. It caused tension and ill-feeling in an otherwise happy and loving relationship and I know that, if things had continued as they were, we would soon have been facing bigger, deeper problems. It was starting the Instagram account that gave us a platform for discussing our money situation and, although I know now that I probably should have raised the conversation in a more direct way before sharing it with thousands of strangers online, it's what helped to crack things open for us. I realize now that some of my posts and articles probably read like open letters to those closest to me, and that's probably essentially what they are.

For us, getting on the same page has been absolutely vital for staying on track – we are now able hold one another to account, and encourage one another to make better decisions. We're not perfect at it, and it takes work – it's especially hard to bring up a potential bump in the road when you've both been feeling that things are going well, but it's necessary.

I have heard from people on both sides of the situation over the course of this year – people with secret debt that not even their partner knows about, and people who have recently found out about a partner's debt. I'm not going to pretend that this is likely to be an easy conversation – of course, when anything has been kept hidden in a relationship, there are questions around trust. I certainly worried about losing the trust of my husband – he had trusted me with the financial security of our family, trusted me with more or less 100% of the salary he worked so hard for, and I felt I had let him down.

The fear of losing a partner over something like debt is crushing, but here's the thing to ask yourself: can you really achieve financial stability and mental wellbeing without having this conversation? Even if you manage to rectify the situation without them ever knowing a thing – which will be very difficult, if they believe you can finance a lifestyle that's actually completely unaffordable – can you live with that?

If the answer to those questions is no, then it's time to talk. The chances are that, if your debt is causing you enough stress for you to have picked up this book, they'll have noticed something's up anyway.

My method for having difficult or daunting conversations is usually to either drink heavily (not advisable here, but this was what I opted for when, in 2014, I needed to tell my now husband that I was sick of being his friend, and that I wanted to be his girlfriend instead) or to get myself into such a nervous state that it all tumbles out in an incoherent jumble, and I have to repeat myself, therefore forcing myself to say it all twice. It's entirely possible that there is no elegant way to start this conversation, but you might consider one of the following options:

Ask your partner to meet you somewhere neutral, tell them there's something serious you need to discuss with them, and ask them to let you finish speaking before responding.

Or

Write them a letter and give it to them to read – making abundantly clear that it is not a *Dear John* before you leave. Email or text are also an option here – only you know how your partner is likely to react to this.

Before you start this conversation, a little bit of preparation is a good idea. Debt charity StepChange advise that you include the following three points when opening up:

- Reassurance that you are dealing with the problem
- An indication of any progress you've made (and I would add, a commitment to further progress)
- A request for them to work with you to make things easier

These can act as a good starting point for what can be an uncomfortable conversation, but I think that it's important to also talk about how you've been feeling as well. Your partner presumably cares for you deeply, and giving the problem context will help them to understand why you haven't felt able to tell them about things before. Also – and it's hard to say this without it coming across as shameless self-promotion – you could use this book as a conversation tool too. You can share any realizations you've had, stories of people who are or have been in the same situation, and you can take them through the plans that you've made using the methods that appear later on.

What I simply cannot tell you is the reaction that your partner is likely to have – they may be calm and understanding from the get-go, it may take them a little longer to come to terms and understand, or there may be some tough times ahead. I do, however, have some insight in the form of others' experiences, which you might find helpful:

My boyfriend proposed, and I didn't want to go into marriage hiding debt or being dishonest about my finances, so I told him about my £13k credit card debt (he knew I had some, but I'd never talked numbers before). I was terrified that he would love me less/think less of me/reject me. He was unphased, loving and supportive. There aren't words to describe the relief I feel to still be loved and that it's not a secret any more.

Last time I sent you a message, I was at breaking point and I thanked you for making me see that I wasn't alone. Since then, I have spoken to my partner about my debt and, although it was bad, it could have been worse. Opening up to my family and partner made me feel lighter and less anxious than I have in years, not to mention gave me help to pau off a credit card balance in full. I still have £800 to pay on a catalogue account and £200 overdraft so I'm not debt free, but I can certainly see the light at the end of the tunnel.

I mentioned before that I have heard from people on both sides of this conversation, and I have seen the hurt and shock caused, not by the debt, but by the secrecy. In spite of that, not a single person who messaged me with their story of finding out about their partner's secret debt had disowned them, or stopped loving them. They used the word 'we' when they talked about solving the problem, and they showed understanding and compassion.

Talking to your family

I'll start with parents – or parent, in my case. In all honesty, I have no idea how I would have gone about telling my dad about my debt. I've imagined the conversation over and over, but what I've come to realize is that I really can't know how it would have gone. It's been almost ten years since he died and I have no idea how close we would be, if I might have confided in him or sought his advice before getting to this point, or how his continued presence in my life might have shaped my approach to money. After almost a decade of convincing myself that his reaction would have been one of extreme disappointment, I feel like this is some sort of progress.

The point I'm trying to make is that how you approach this conversation very much depends on your parents' personalities, and the type of relationship you have with them as an adult. It may be that you find it easier to open up to one than the other, and it's fine to just sit down with whomever you feel most comfortable with, to begin with – there doesn't have to be a family meeting or *How I Met Your Mother*-style intervention, complete with banner. You actually don't really have to tell your parents, but if you need emotional or financial support, it could be a good idea – they can't help you if they don't know you're struggling.

Of course, not everyone has a typical parent-child relationship with their folks. Some of us are closer to other family members, and therefore rely on them more for support and sometimes financial help. Neither my husband nor I have access to what the newspapers glibly refer to as 'The Bank of Mum & Dad', but both as a family and in our previous, single lives, we have been helped out to the tune of thousands by a whole host of relatives.

One of the biggest challenges when opening up to family, in my experience, is that, in the very vast majority of cases, they will have already helped you out financially to some degree. Obviously, your parents (or whomever you lived with growing up) will have quite literally paid for your entire existence until you were old enough to work, and sometimes beyond, but what I'm really talking about here are the leg-ups and the bail-outs. There is something uniquely awful about the prospect of saying to a family member – usually someone you love very much – 'I know you helped me, but I'm still in this position'.

Unless you're going to be relying on family for help out of an urgent sticky situation – no judgement here, lots of us have had to call on relatives to make our rent or childcare bill more than once – you can afford to bide your time a little on this one. If you can make a little headway in your plans for a better financial future, you can present your situation alongside a clear method for sorting it out, and it just might make it that little bit easier to talk about.

Of course, you might not find family members from different generations – particularly those who fall under the 'Baby Boomer' umbrella – or with completely different circumstances are understanding to begin with. There is always the possibility that they will judge you, but I hope that everything you've learned so far in this book – the unique challenges of our generation, the link between money and mental health and the trap of emotional spending – has equipped you to better question that attitude, or at least to stop you from absorbing and internalizing that judgement as shame. There is always an opportunity, when you open up to other generations, to educate even as you seek help.

You may, of course, be pleasantly surprised to find that your dad/grandad/aunt has also made some financial mistakes during the course of their lifetime, and that they understand a lot better than you think. Or that they simply understand that things *were* a little easier before the 2008 crash, and that they recognize that money management is about more than just cash in your wallet or numbers on a screen. Stranger things have happened.

Talking to friends

Grown-up friendships are fantastic, but they are plagued by a whole raft of complications that aren't generally solved by a 'sorry' note passed in class or a quick scuffle in the playground. One of those can be our tendency to compare ourselves and the milestones we've reached with our friends, particularly those who we have grown up with – who we were once on a level pegging with as we embarked on our adult lives. As we fall into different careers, start making different salaries, choose different partners and make other life decisions, we lose the ability to talk openly without sometimes feeling that we're being dragged into some kind of hierarchy – who's doing the best, and who's flagging behind. This all happens very much under the surface, of course, but it can make it extraordinarily difficult to admit to any setbacks in the big plan, for fear of losing your place in the subconscious pecking order.

I am phenomenally lucky to have a group of six very close female friends. We have laughed, cried, counselled and gossiped our way through the last fifteen years or so. We talk about everything. But I didn't tell a single one of them about the financial worries that were weighing down on me so heavily. Not when I struggled to contribute to joint birthday gifts, not when I had to bail out of holidays. We don't live in the same city any more and I have young children, so saying no to Friday night drinks wasn't such a problem, but I know that I still would have struggled to confide in them and would have felt the need to carry on pretending that everything was fine.

In May last year, I sent this text to our group chat:

Girls . . . something quite bonkers is happening to me and I wanted to wait and tell you all about it when I saw you but I think I need to tell you now.

Basically, thanks to two lots of maternity leave, the wedding, childcare etc and basically always having been shit with money, Phil and I have a LOT of credit card debt. A lot. Like £25k. It's OK, and we're going to be able to pay it back fairly quickly, we're not struggling any more and everything is FINE. But back in March things got quite hairy and I knew we needed to get a handle on it, so I started an Instagram account to basically hold myself to account. A few people started to take notice and I've done a couple of interviews for things, and I wrote a piece for a popular blog . . . fast forward a couple of weeks and my account now has over 10k followers, and I'm being asked to do some amazing things.

I can't believe this is all happening to me and I wanted to talk to you all about it sooner, but you are all so sensible with money and doing so well that I felt a bit ashamed to open up about it . . . I know it's silly but I'm even a bit nervous sending this message! I hope you don't all think I'm a stupid idiot.

Surprisingly, it just about fitted within the limit for one message. My heart was pounding as I sent it, and when I read it now I can see the panic in every line. *Please don't hate me. Please don't pity me. I'm still just me.* I can see where I've glossed over things, emphasized the positives, not given them a beat to ask any questions – but sometimes that's what you have to do to open up the conversation.

Their reaction was, of course, to be massively supportive. There were some awkward questions, and I'm sure not every thought that flashed through their minds was positive. One friend was hurt that I hadn't confided sooner. Another expressed her reservations about me ever forfeiting my anonymity. But another opened up about some struggles she'd been having recently too, and the hush around the subject of money in our group has all but disappeared since then.

I have newer and less close friends that I've started to open up to too, a reference to credit cards here, a declined invitation or suggestion for something cheaper to do there. I've been massively surprised by how willing people often are to talk about their own finances once you start the conversation – of the generous handful of people I've mentioned our credit card issues to, only on one or two haven't immediately referred to their own loan or credit card balance. I no longer feel the need to pretend we can afford several different hobbies for our children, or that we're just on the verge of buying a house. Those things have materially helped not only my mental wellbeing, but also our actual financial situation, in that we no longer fork out a fortune for the sake of keeping up with the Joneses. That recognition that 'The Joneses' are either your friends, in which case they probably don't care that you've stopped doing Rugby Tots or that you don't have a cleaner, or they're people whose opinion shouldn't really matter that much to you.

Broaching the subject with friends – unless you want to try a sudden bombshell text like me – can be as simple as saying 'We can't make drinks, sorry. We're trying to pay off our credit card so things are a bit tight right now,', or as complicated as a deep chat about the emotional complexities of your relationship with money – it really depends on how close you are, the dynamic of your friendship and how ready you are to talk about things. There can be tendency amongst friends to minimize financial worries with a cheeky wink, perhaps wanting to hold on to the days when being broke meant not having managed to swipe enough change to get the bus up to the cinema, and it takes a special kind of strength to say no to that 'Oh, go onnnnn' when you know there's twenty quid left on your credit card limit. Opening up properly can help to combat that, if you're ready and the trust is there.

What to say if . . .

- Someone pulls the 'some people are worse off so stop moaning' card:
  This is a frustrating comment in any situation, and it applies to almost everyone in Western culture. A good approach here is to acknowledge your privilege, but point out that sleepless nights and panic attacks, struggling to pay your bills and having no money for quality of life is a legitimate problem.

- Someone asks why you didn't 'just stop spending':
  A calm explanation of the fact that money management, and knowing when you can afford to treat yourself, is quite a difficult skill when it doesn't come naturally. Explaining the emotional factors in spending, and the specific triggers you've faced, can help too. Please also

feel free to point them in the direction of the mental health chapter in this book.

- Someone calls you irresponsible:
  This is a great time to demonstrate all of the areas of your life where you successfully manage intense responsibilities – keeping your children alive, or holding down a job, for example. It can also be worth saying that you recognize you've done some irresponsible things in the past, but that you're making changes now.

Oh, and in case I haven't made it clear enough that you don't really owe anyone an explanation, a hard stare and a swift change of subject is also a perfectly reasonable response.

Talking to your bank and creditors

If you're struggling to keep your head above water, or have debt and are unable to make your minimum repayments, the last thing you probably want to do is speak to your bank or credit card company. But the reality is that speaking to people in a wide variety of financial situations is literally their job, and there's no need to be embarrassed at all. It's a bit like going to your GP with some kind of genital peculiarity – you're utterly mortified, but they see this kind of shit all the time.

It takes courage to pick up the phone, but you can just as easily send a letter or email, and if there's one thing I've learned in the last year, it's that writing it all down can be cathartic. In general, I've found some lenders to be more helpful and sympathetic than others, but even when I ended a conversation feeling frustrated that there was nothing the advisor could or would do to help, I at least knew that *I* had done something – that I had taken action where the easier option would have just been to cast it to the back of my mind.

The sooner you feel ready to have these conversations, the sooner you will know what help is available to you, and how it might enable you to break the cycle of living pay day to pay day, chip away at your debt or stop falling into an unarranged overdraft that bit quicker. Again, you may feel you want to earmark a particular day to speak to all of your lenders, and that can work, but remember that explaining your situation over and over, and often having to challenge the first responses you get, can be emotionally taxing. You may prefer to speak to everyone over the course of a week or longer, giving yourself time to recover, process and learn from the results of the previous conversation. It's totally up to you, but I'm going to run through an example of how these things often go, with a little bit of a script to keep you on track, especially as I know how hard it is not to let the tears flow when you're struggling to make yourself heard.

Step One: Decide what would help you

It's really good to have a clear idea of what you want your bank to do for you before you pick up the phone. What would be most helpful for you is entirely dependent on your individual circumstances, so think carefully about what you're looking to achieve. Here are a few of the things that your bank or credit card company may be able to do for you without you needing to enter into an official Payment Arrangement Plan (we'll discuss these a little bit later on, as they can really ease some pressure but do affect your credit file):

- **Offer financial advice**
  If your money worries don't stem from debt, but you feel you're either heading in that direction or treading water, most banks can offer free advice on how to achieve your financial goals, and will tell you about services that may help you. Just be aware that they may be looking to sell you a financial product, like a fee-paying bank account, so it may be worth having a policy of not agreeing to anything straight away and giving yourself some time to think.

- **Reduce your interest rate**
  If you're on a high rate but have a decent credit score, your lender may be able to put you on a better rate without you needing to do a balance transfer.

- **Refund fees and charges**
  Bank penalty charges and credit card late payment fees can really compound any financial issues you are having, but

the good news is that having these charges removed and refunded might be as easy as asking. I was in a mess of bounced payments and late fees for a long time, and I've never had an advisor refuse to remove them. If all you need is a little change of direction, a little bounce back on to the right path, then this can really help.

- **Refund or freeze interest as a goodwill gesture**
There are a few banks who, if you're struggling with high interest on a high balance, but showing that you're committed to paying it off, will agree to simply freeze or refund interest for a month or two if they're not able to offer you a better rate.

Step two: Get everything prepared, and pick up the phone

As obvious as this might sound, having everything set up for the conversation beforehand can really help. If you're feeling nervous, get a bit of fresh air. Make sure you have all of your account details to hand (or if you've thrown away/hidden all of your paperwork, some identifying details), make yourself a drink and make sure your phone is fully charged if using a mobile. Don't run out of battery halfway through and then have to explain the whole thing to someone new – take it from someone who knows! I have also frequently had these calls with one or both of my children asking for snacks and falling over. Again, this isn't ideal as you can miss important information – try to avoid if possible.

Here's a little script that might help to start you off with asking the right questions, based on my own experience:

~~Coldplay~~ *Terrible hold music finally clicks off*

Advisor: Hello, you're through to *Scary Bank*, how can I help?

You: Hello, I'd like to discuss some charges/the interest rate on my account with you please.

Advisor: Okay, what is it you'd like to discuss?

You: Well, I have had some problems with cashflow and missed a payment/entered into an unarranged overdraft. As a result, you've applied charges to my account, and I was wondering if you might be so kind as to refund them?

or

You: Well, I have quite a large balance on my account with you, and the high interest rate is making it very difficult for me to make headway into paying it off. Are there any lower rates that you can offer me to help with this?

At this point, the advisor will probably ask to put you on hold while they see what they can do for you. Penalty charges are usually a fairly quick solve, as most advisors are authorized to do this themselves.

Interest rates can take a little longer, and if you're struggling with your credit rating, then the better rates – I've known people to have their reduced from 18% to 6% before – may be out of your grasp. You may be pleasantly surprised by the result of your interest enquiry, or you may be feeling a little disappointed that your sky-high rate remains. If the latter is the case, there's still one last thing to try for, which is an interest freeze or refund as a gesture of good will. Banks often won't offer this as a matter of course, so you will probably have to push a little – something along the lines of:

'That's disappointing to hear. Is there anything else that you can offer to help me in my commitment to reducing my balance? Are you able to freeze or refund any interest at all to help me make a dent in this? Anything you can offer to help would be much appreciated.'

Step 3: Stay calm, if you can

I fully understand the temptation, or sometimes irresistible urge, to cry. My voice has wobbled through these conversations on many occasions, but it really helps to stay calm. It can be very frustrating if all you get is a flat 'computer says no', but remember that no matter how cold the advisor may sound, it is entirely possible that their hands are genuinely tied. It's also worth noting that the person you're speaking to is a human being with their own life and own problems too. I used to feel quite judged and patronized when speaking to advisors on the phone – I would assume that they were looking at my numbers on their screen and feeling superior, and it would make me both embarrassed and angry. But since starting my Instagram account, I've heard from dozens of people working as bank or mortgage advisors who have financial difficulties of their own. The have told me how they feel like frauds, how ashamed they are, and how terrified that somebody from work will find out and their job will be at risk. Just some food for thought.

Step 4: Use this as a starting point

It's easy, as life takes over, to forget the hard work and emotional investment that goes into these triumphs and let them get filed away with other things that you started and didn't finish. It's important to resist that now. It doesn't matter whether you've managed to get what you wanted from your bank – you've done something really brave. Don't let your inner critic minimize that, because that act of courage can be the start of real change. In having that conversation, despite the nerves, the anxiety and the pain, you have engaged with progress. Use it to propel you forward – don't be despondent if you didn't get the result you wanted, or complacent if you did. From a cynical perspective, your lender is not really offering you a lower rate because they want to help you to clear your debt – they are offering it to keep you spending. But it's up to you whether you use it to your own ends, or to theirs.

Further help from your bank

During the course of these conversations, if they feel it would help, your bank or lender may offer to put you through to someone in their financial difficulties team. Following new legislation in 2018, creditors are obliged to help customers who they perceive to be in 'persistent debt', which is defined as debt where, over a period of eighteen months, the amount they pay in interest, fees and charges is more than the amount of debt they repay.[3]

Whether you take them up on this offer is entirely up to you. We'll speak a bit more about the help that's available if you feel that you're in completely over your head a little later, but if you're struggling to make minimum repayments or there's the wrong kind of gap between your income and outgoings, your bank's financial difficulties team can be a good place to start. The advisors on this team are specially trained to advise on tougher and more persistent money problems, so you may want to seek their advice, even if you don't want to pursue any of the measures that they can put in place.

One of the things that they may be able to offer is a Payment Arrangement Plan. This is where interest may be frozen, and your monthly repayment amount reduced to an affordable amount. Someone will be able to go through your monthly income, outgoings and other financial commitments with you in order to help you to work out what's affordable for you, and you can decide whether to go ahead with the plan. Paying less than the minimum amount, even if agreed with your bank, will be visible to lenders on your credit file and make getting credit more difficult, but it may be worth sacrificing access to more credit, especially if you're struggling to manage your current debts, for the peace of mind that affordable repayments will give you.

If you are at crisis point

If you've done the sums and the amount seems completely insurmountable, or if you've had a recent change in your circumstances that means that you simply can't afford even the minimum repayments, there is no amount of clever budgeting or cutting back on luxuries that is going to make a difference. This would be defined as 'problem debt', and it is likely to be taking a huge toll on your mental, emotional and physical wellbeing. Now is the time to seek help – but the good news is that this kind of help is readily available and free of charge.

If you have multiple creditors, and the job of negotiating with each of them individually feels overwhelming, there are other options that can help you to take back control and also preserve your own mental health. Debt charities like StepChange[4] offer excellent advice and support, as well as practical solutions that can help you to reduce your repayments and clear your debt, particularly if you're at crisis point. They can often negotiate with your creditors for you, allowing you some vital breathing space and removing some of the worry that comes with juggling multiple accounts. There's no commitment to starting any kind of plan when you contact them, but they can help you to decide which might be best for you, whether that's a Debt Management Plan (DMP), an Individual Voluntary Arrangement (IVA), Debt Relief Order (DRO) or bankruptcy. Some of these terms may sound scary, and entering into any of these agreements will have implications for your credit file, but there's absolutely no shame in seeking help of this sort. These schemes can be your pathway to a better and happier life, which, at the end of the day, is sort of the ultimate goal for us all. Recently, someone sent me the following message about their experience of debt intervention:

> This week we have been declared insolvent and it is like a huge weight lifted. We never fell behind in payments, but have struggled to make any real progress with our debt. We were so ashamed, we didn't feel like we deserved help, especially since we could technically cover payments. I'd love people to know that every debt helpline we talked to, everyone has treated us with so much kindness, respect and patience. It wish we had done it sooner! It's not the ending we hoped for, but it has given us so much more hope and a much brighter financial (and mental health) future.

Important: if you've looked for solutions online, or checked your credit score, you may be served adverts on other websites or Facebook for debt-relief services. Most of these

charge a fee, and many have questionable credentials. **Debt charities (see the back of this book) offer all of the same services, but with no fee, and their teams are staffed by experts who will help you to make this manageable.**

So, if you have debt that feels overwhelming, please know that help is there, and that it's not an admission of failure to accept that you need assistance in rebuilding your finances. It doesn't mean the end of your dreams of owning a home or being able to build a financially secure future – in fact, it may just provide the platform you need to make that possible.

Is debt always bad?

The answer to that question depends entirely on who you ask. In general, in the UK, student loans and mortgages are seen as completely acceptable debt by most – mainly because there are only around five people in the whole country who could pay cash for a house or a university education. Other debt retains a weird stigma, which is odd given that quite so many of us have such a lot of it, and that it's advertised so freely and often aggressively.

Before we start to set goals, it's worth thinking about our own personal attitude towards debt, and what we're comfortable with on a personal level. Much of the literature out there is incredibly all-or-nothing on the subject of debt, and there's a lot of emphasis on that coveted 'debt-free' status.

As I have repeatedly said throughout this book, the takeaway from this should not necessarily be a commitment to never taking out another credit product again – it should be the ability to be on top of our finances and remain in calm control of our income and outgoings. I may always have a car on finance, or I may sometimes use a credit card for a big purchase in future – but the point is that, once we reach a point of control over our financial wellbeing, we can make those decisions based on sense rather than emotions. We can decide to take on a manageable, affordable amount of debt, if we know that it won't have implications for our mental and emotional health. Once we free ourselves from the cycle, we can enter into those relationships with a plan for repayment and a clear idea of what we are borrowing for, rather than accepting credit from whoever will give it to us, and watching it disappear on nothing.

A word of caution: payday loans

While I'm not going to talk you through every type of credit available to you – there are plenty of places that will help you to weigh up the pros and cons of loans and credit cards – I feel this particular type of lending needs flagging up. Short-term, high-interest loans, often known as payday loans, are bad news. The rates of interest can be absolutely astronomical, but they are often marketed as the perfect solution to short-term cashflow problems – you know the advert: woman tries to start car, checks bank balance, looks sad, goes on to shorttermsolution.com and all of a sudden everything is fine. The cash is in her account within the hour so that she can pay her mechanic and drive to work, easy-peasy.

What these adverts don't show, of course, is the financial difficulty caused the following month, when her family are scrambling to make the repayments. What they also don't show is the shaking head of their mortgage advisor when, a year down the line, they are trying to buy a house or re-mortgage their current home, and nobody will lend to them because they've used this service.

Following a lot of scrutiny, and new regulations from the Financial Conduct Authority, payday loans have evolved since I was stuck in a cycle of paying Wonga a steadily increasing percentage of my salary each month, then borrowing more to make up the shortfall. The new wave of high-cost short-term credit providers allow you to spread repayments over a number of months rather than paying it back all in one lump sum, and they are obliged to make it abundantly clear to borrowers what the overall cost of their loan will be. But they are still targeting vulnerable people – often people with bad credit, who are already struggling to manage their finances – who need quick access to cash, and in my opinion their affordability checks are nowhere near stringent enough. An example from one of these short-term lenders shows that, if you were to borrow £480 and repay it over a period of nine months, you would end up repaying £959.04 in total.[5]

Any kind of high-interest short-term loan is a serious undertaking, which is belied by the fact that you can get hold of one with a few taps on your phone. They should be treated with absolute caution and used only as a very last resort. Without meaning to scare anyone who has ever had one – it's not the actual end of the world – here is an account from somebody who has been held back by using a payday loan instead of borrowing elsewhere:

> *I've just found out that I can't move home and get a new mortgage because of a payday loan I took out last year. I had no idea how hugely harmful one mistake could be and the huge effect it would have on my future. At the time, I felt too embarrassed to speak to my family about my money problems and saw it as a short-term solution.*

The fact that incomes are so stretched for many people in the UK, coupled with a reluctance to talk about money worries that is so strong that we would rather pay these eye-watering rates than ask for help, has created the perfect environment for unethical lenders to thrive. By owning our financial situation, shedding the associated shame and speaking openly about things, we lessen their power. I hope to one day see them disappear altogether.

Having reached the end of this chapter, you should feel more empowered and informed, and ready for the next step. I hope that you have been able to decide what help and support you need – whether that be from those close to you, from your bank or from an organisation like StepChange. If you need to take some time to process the outcomes of all of these conversations, take it – you can do this at your own pace. The next chapter will help you to lay some practical foundations for your path towards financial control, and to get organized – a vital step that I skipped in every previous failed attempt to get on top of things.

Eight
Getting Ready

It's tempting, once you've made the leap and started addressing your money worries, to dive straight in with the first regime that springs to mind. From someone who has tried and failed to fix their finances that way many times in the past, please don't do that. In order for you to succeed in making lasting changes, this next step needs to be about making sure that your budget is right for your circumstances and that your goals are achievable for you. We've all seen the American debt-payoff stories, where someone holds up a board saying that they've paid off $90,000 in just over twenty minutes or something, but these stories of insanely quick successes are a red herring – they are completely unachievable for most of us, and they'll only serve to make you feel worse.

When I first calculated what I owed, I knew that I wasn't in a position to do much about it right there and then, so I used the time to plan. Financial planning for you as an individual, couple or family isn't just about numbers. It goes far deeper than that.

This chapter will help you to lay the foundations of your own, personal financial journey. It will help you to set goals, and come up with a budget to help you to achieve them. It will help you to decide the right plan for paying off your debt and give you the toolkit you need to do so.

How to set goals that won't end up haunting you

When I was younger, I treated setting goals as a way to be unkind to myself. It would involve picking out all of the things I didn't like about myself, and then creating a list of gruelling instructions for how I needed to change them. Back then, they were mainly about diet and exercise, or university work, but I see the same thing within the Debt Free Community on Instagram on the first of each month. Goal-setting is, in itself, a very positive thing, but the pressure that I see people putting themselves under to keep their food shop within a tiny budget or to make a certain amount of money through side hustles makes me feel uncomfortable. These are the same goals that I see reposted mid-month with a 'failed' stamp across them, and a self-abusing caption that makes me wish I could reach out and give them a hug. It makes me wonder how many times this will happen before that person gives up.

Our goals shouldn't exist as a stick to beat ourselves with, they should be the carrot with which we encourage ourselves to engage in more positive behaviour, and our motivation to keep going when things don't seem to be happening quickly enough. They should paint a picture of the future that we want for ourselves, but be realistic enough that we can create a path to take us there. (As someone who, at one point, was genuinely convinced that I was going to meet and marry Robert Pattinson, I need you to trust me when I say that setting achievable goals is important.)

The first thing that we need to consider, when we set both short- and long-term goals, is the big picture. What do we want in life in general? For most of us, the answer to this question is the same. We want to feel happy, fulfilled and secure. We want to feel equipped to deal with whatever life throws at us. So simple.

We can then filter that down into some individual goals. In order to do that, we need to think about what it would take for us to achieve that elusive big-picture ideal, and set long-term goals accordingly. When I set my own after a couple of months of paying off debt, I realized how helpful it would have been to have them from the start. They have helped me to stay on track when it's seemed that my financial freedom is slipping from my grasp, or when the slog has seemed frustratingly slow and boring. They have helped me to stay hopeful and positive.

I also realized that it's important to link them back to that ultimate goal of happiness, because sometimes it makes us realize that the things we thought we wanted aren't necessarily what's going to make us happy. Yours will likely be different, and there's space for you to set them in a moment, but I'll share mine:

Long-term goals

Goal:
To reach a point where we have enough time together as a family, but are also each able to pursue something that makes us feel fulfilled outside of work and home life.

How it will make me happier:
Family is important to me, and quality time together makes me happy. I sometimes feel that I have no time for myself, to do things that I enjoy, and this detracts from my happiness.

Goal:
To own a home where:

- My children can play safely, inside and outside
- Keeping things clean and tidy is achievable
- We are able to have friends round, and have family to stay

How it will make me happier:
The stability of owning a home rather than renting is important to me. I know the frustrations of trying to keep my children safe and my home tidy in a house with an impractical layout, and that is not what I choose for my future. Seeing our friends makes us happy, and our extended family live a distance away – being able to host them would mean we could see them more often.

> **Goal:**
> To be credit card- and loan-debt free as our default position,
> and have some modest savings for security
>
> **How this will make me happier:**
> I have come to realize that financial security for me is vital
> for my happiness. Being free of the anxiety that comes with
> debt, and knowing that we have a safety net, will give us
> peace of mind and enable us to focus on other things
> instead of worrying all the time.

So, as you can see, these are quite big goals, each of which I can
identify as being key to my future happiness and security. Now
you try:

> ## Long-term goals
>
> **Goal:**
>
>
> **How it will make me happier:**
>
>
> **Goal:**
>
>
> **How it will make me happier:**

Once we have set our long-term goals, it becomes easier to look at the more incremental things we need to achieve in order to get there. Even though only one of the goals I've listed above relates directly to money, all three require an improvement in my finances in order to be achievable. In order for us to have enough time together as a family, my husband will need to have the freedom to pursue a career that doesn't mean working antisocial hours. In order to buy a house, we will need to save for a number of years.

How frequently you set short-term goals is up to you. You can use them to set yourself little challenges, like taking a packed lunch to work every day for a week, picking up the phone to your creditors or not using your credit card that month. You can use them alongside your budget to set savings or debt payoff targets. Whatever you like – just try to ensure that they are feeding into your bigger goals, and therefore your ultimate goal.

There isn't space in this book to give you a box to fill in every week or month, but all you really need for this is a pen and some paper, or your notes app. Revisit them to check your progress, but don't fall into the self-flagellation trap if something has held you back from achieving them. Self-loathing is pretty much the opposite of the ultimate goal, after all.

How to budget without ruining your life

Can you think of a less sexy word than 'budget'? To me, it's always conjured up images of night after night of Tesco Value beans in their blue-and-white stripy tin, and of having to say no to anything remotely fun. But I think budgets actually *can* be a bit sexy. I'll explain why.

We need to stop thinking of a budget as being something that exists to restrict us, of it being imposed on us by an external force. We need to think of it as our own personal plan for staying in control of our finances, and something in which we very much have the final say. It can feel daunting to get it all down on paper, but remember that, in laying the situation out in front of us, we're not changing any of the numbers. Your income and fixed outgoings will be the same, whether you're paying attention or not – so isn't it better to have that visibility? To be able to make a conscious decision about where any disposable income is going, rather than letting it slip through your fingers?

The most life-changing part of looking back over my income and outgoings over the last year was exposing a fundamental flaw in my budgeting technique. There was a layer of haze between what I though was going on and what was really happening. Because I was often scared to look at the numbers with any degree of clarity, there was always a degree of fudging and overlap that went on. I would round income up and outgoings down, because it made me feel better at the time. I would overestimate the impact of extra income and under-estimate the effect of a new bill. Those little discrepancies every month add up over time. Knowledge isn't power if you choose to ignore it and do things your own way anyway.

My budgeting technique is not revolutionary, nor does it come from a place of expertise or fiscal know-how. It comes from a place of knowing what has worked for me, and of wanting to offer you something accessible and straightforward.

Step 1: Examine your spending patterns

I have found that a necessary step in making a successful budget is to look at your past spending behaviour in detail. To get an idea of a typical month, you should look back over the course of a six-month period or more – just to make sure you're not basing your budget on an outlier. You might wince at how much you've spent on that sauvignon blanc you like, or how many trips to the Co-Op you make on a weekly basis, but it's impossible to know what you can and can't cut out or reduce in your outgoings without looking at where you're spending, and why.

The why is important, because unless you can tackle the root cause, you'll find it really difficult to make any lasting changes. For instance, if you've cringed at your monthly takeaway bill, but the reason you're ordering in is that you can never find the time or energy to cook, you need to address that and find new ways to cope. If you simply vow to cut out the takeaways and plan to make some complicated, wholesome meal instead, there's a very real possibility that you'll get in from work that day with absolutely nothing left in the tank, and before you know it, the chow mein is on its way and the ingredients for your Thai curry are left to go off in the fridge. Then, not only will you have spent more than you originally would have, what with having bought dinner twice, but you'll feel like shit about it too. We'll talk meal planning later, but this is just an example of one of the many ways you can get things wrong in your budget, if you forget to apply it in the context of your everyday life.

If you have a number of different accounts to look at, like I did, an app like Money Dashboard, which enables you to add all of your accounts and look at your historical spending as a whole, can be useful. You can also use it to track your spending going forward – it's what I use, but there are a number of different apps for this kind of thing on the market.

Step 2: Look at your income and fixed outgoings

This bit is more or less straight-up maths. I do my budget in a fairly simple spreadsheet that's designed to give me all the information I need to make things work. The formulas are all really simple, because it's mainly adding and subtracting, so it would be fairly easy to build something similar yourself. Otherwise, there are dozens of templates online, some of which I've indicated at the end of this chapter.

For anyone with a consistent, salaried income, or for families with two, you simply need to calculate how much money you're bringing in on a monthly basis, and treat that as your starting point. This is how much money you have in your pot at the start of the month, and your job now is to make every pound work for you.

For families with one or more person who is self-employed, this is a little more complicated. As someone who is newly self-employed themselves, I enter the minimum that I know I will be able to contribute on our main bill date every month. Another method, once you've been working for yourself for a while, is to pay yourself the same 'salary' every month out of your 'business pot'. I'm not an expert on this – in fact, I definitely fall into the category of freelance rookie, but there are some excellent resources out there for self-employed people.

Your fixed outgoings are the things you can't live without, and can't change, like your rent, council tax and any other payments that stay the same every month. Childcare also falls into this category, but one of the many reasons childcare costs can throw you off is that they can vary from month to month. I approach this by calculating my childcare costs a few months ahead, and filling them in ahead of time. Just as a warning, five-week months might leave you wanting to run for the hills.

If your fixed outgoings exceed your income, please flip back a few pages and consider getting in touch with a money advice service – there really is no way to budget your way out of that situation.

Note: At this stage, it might be useful to look at whether there are some essentials that you could be paying a little less for, such as your utility bills. There are some excellent services for this available – my preferred option being Moneysavingexpert. com's Cheap Energy Club.[1]

Step 3: Consider your other regular outgoings

These are bills that are not necessarily essential living costs, but which contribute to your quality of life, such as any entertainment packages, memberships or subscriptions you might have. You might feel tempted to strip these out completely, but it's worth considering the value that they bring to your life. You probably don't need to be subscribed to three different TV streaming services, but can you really imagine living without Netflix for as long as it takes you to achieve your financial goals? You're a better person than me if you can make it through the winter without open access to terrible rom-coms and binge-worthy boxsets.

So, my approach here was to look at what I would miss, and what I wouldn't. Anything on the 'wouldn't miss' list was cancelled immediately. Then I considered what I could go without for a period of time, while I tried to get us back on a level-pegging, but that I would want to reintroduce at some point, and cancelled or put them on hold. This is another misconception of budgeting that I think can be off-putting – that it's set in stone, and you have to follow the same plan from the moment you get started to the moment you reach your destination. Your budget should flex in time with the undulations of your life. More on this later.

Step 4: Examine your variable expenses

These are things that change every month, such as your food or petrol bill. Although they are essential to living, we have some degree of control over what we spend on them. An eye-opener here is often what we spend on food. We can spend what we feel is a reasonable amount on the weekly shop, but forget that those top-ups add up. Think about how you might be able to reduce these without setting yourself impossible tasks – there is no point in planning to switch your supermarket to Aldi if your nearest one is ten miles away.

Step 5: Look at what's left

Once you've taken out essential living costs and non-negotiables, what you're left with is your resources for paying off debt, saving and enjoyment, and it's your choice as to how you allocate those funds. It might well take you a few months to work out the right balance, and that's okay.

Of course, when it comes to debt repayments, there will be a minimum amount that you need to pay every month to stay on top of your account, the sum of which depends on how much you owe and how many creditors you have. Strategies for repaying debt are covered in the next section, but if repaying debt is a priority for you, this is probably where you'll want to allocate most of your disposable income. There is something to be said for putting away a small amount in savings every month, however, and leaving some budget for enjoyment too. I have an allocation of roughly £200 per month for doing things with the kids and an occasional curry or trip to Nandos. Balancing this correctly is, I think, the key to a successful budget.

Don't crash budget

I did warn you that there'd be dieting analogies . . . In the same way that I fully understand the allure of a crash diet, I know that the appeal of stripping out every extra cost from your budget can be hard to resist, especially if you're angry with yourself. But punitive budgeting just doesn't work in the long run, because you grow resentful and bitter as you start to feel more and more deprived. If we take things right back to our goal of happiness, security and mental wellbeing, months and possibly years on end of putting your life on hold for the sake of improving your finances doesn't really make sense. After all, to put a slightly morbid spin on the matter, you could finish off paying your debt or reach your savings goal, and promptly get hit by a bus.

That's not to say that it's not healthy or necessary to make a few sacrifices – after all, if we carry on doing the exact same things, we can only expect the exact same outcome – but making sure we keep our emotional wellbeing front of mind is important.

A realist's approach to meal planning

Virtually nobody has the time, energy or patience to prepare elaborate meals from scratch every single day, and we all forget to pick up a vital ingredient or take the chicken out of the freezer from time to time. Food is often a downfall in people's budgets, and I can absolutely see why – it's very easy to underestimate what you and your family consume in a week, and if you're in the habit of just 'popping' out for things, you can end up spending an absolute fortune at your local Tesco Express.

I find meal-planning a really helpful tool in reducing not only what we spend, but what we waste. However, as with almost every other element of this lifestyle change, I have found that it's necessary to allow a certain degree of flex for the 'real life' factor. When I first started meal-planning, I was far too ambitious, and far too rigid. I would find that meals went unmade as either I was too exhausted to cook them, or they just weren't what we fancied that night. Because we were using mainly fresh ingredients, our food bill was higher, and the risk of things going off before we'd had the chance to eat them was higher too, so we had to have a re-think. This is the importance of allowing space for learning in every aspect of this journey – previously I would have taken any failure like this to heart, but once I removed the pressure of getting everything absolutely right from the outset, I found that I was able to actually learn what worked for my family. Thinking about the realities of your week – the times when you'll be able to eat together and the days when you'll be grabbing a bite at different times, the days you'll have the time and energy to cook and the days when you won't – will allow you to plan and shop for meals that work with your life.

I started planning a typical week based on three staples cooked from scratch, three very low-effort meals using mainly store-cupboard and freezer food, and one 'special' meal – something cooked from a recipe, or a roast dinner. Because my husband works odd hours, but usually still needs something to eat when he gets home in the middle of the night, a couple of these meals need to be easy to re-heat (and preferably bearable to eat once you've done so).

A typical week might look something like this:

Monday: Prawn Thai noodles
Tuesday: Ham & mushroom risotto
Wednesday: Jacket potato with tuna & cucumber
Thursday: Beans & cheese on toast
Friday: Fish-finger sandwiches
Saturday: Chicken stroganoff
Sunday: Roast pork

It's a bit boring, but it's reality. There are an absolute wealth of budget cookbooks out there to try – Jack Monroe and Miguel Barclay being two of my favourite budget conscious cooks – and recipes that you can access for free online. It's just worth factoring in the time, energy and washing up, as well as the cost per serving. Because if it's still in the fridge while you eat a chicken tikka masala, it's not helping you towards your financial goals.

The importance of saving – even if you have debt

As I have mentioned a couple of times previously, having savings is an important part of feeling financially secure – it helps us to feel less vulnerable to events outside of our control, and also to feel that we are building something, that we are growing towards our goals. Until very recently, I had assumed that all savings should just be put aside into one big pot, but having set some concrete goals, I now realize how much more sense it makes to divide savings into separate pots, and give each a specific job to do.

For me, this means dividing anything I save into three. The first pot is to ensure that I have the funds to cover any unexpected expenses – an 'emergency fund'. The second is to go towards specific, short-term goals or events, such as Christmas, holidays, or the 900 weddings that I have been invited to since I turned thirty. The third is to go towards my long-term goals – namely, buying a house. How to allocate any money you have earmarked for saving is entirely up to you, and you can make it as simple or as complicated as you like. There is a whole world of different savings accounts to explore, each with features that make them more or less suitable for different types of savings, but the important thing is to decide what your goals are, and ensure that any saving method is helping you towards them.

If ever I have talked to a proper 'money person' about my attitude towards saving alongside paying off debt, they've looked at me like I've gone completely mad. And, if we were looking at this journey in purely logical terms, they might have a point. The interest you accrue on most savings accounts is minuscule compared to the interest you pay on most credit accounts, it's true, and based purely on numbers, the logical thing to do would be to allocate every spare penny towards your debt. And yet, there is something about the psychological benefits of growing something positive, rather than just diminishing something negative, that makes me sure that saving a small amount while you pay off debt is a good idea.

I'll concede that it makes no sense to focus your main efforts on saving, especially if your debt is as big as mine, but creating a fund for planned treats and emergencies makes sense for a number of reasons. As long as you share my belief that people paying off debt or experiencing financial difficulty also deserve to have nice things and experiences, you must be able to see that saving up for those things makes far more sense than paying all available funds towards a credit card for months, then using said credit card to pay for a mini-break. Similarly, if the safety net for unexpected bills is a credit card, the emotional impact of working so hard, for so long, to reduce the balance, only to see it shoot up again, is massive. It feels like going backwards, and it runs the risk of derailing you entirely.

You might also want to save a little towards your long-term goals, as a sort of statement of faith in their achievability. Every now and then, I will slip a little bit of money into my Lifetime ISA (a bit like a Help to Buy ISA), and it feels like a promise to myself.

There are ways in which you can save without derailing your debt payoff progress. Savings challenges – where you save small or increasing amounts according to a certain pattern – are popular online right now. But my favourite incremental saving tool is the one where some banks (Halifax, Lloyds and Bank of Scotland, for example) and apps (like Moneybox) automatically round up each debit card transaction and siphon the extra off into a separate account for you. It's slow going, but it adds up.

Getting into the habit of saving, even when your main efforts are focussed on paying off debt, can only be a good thing.

Your digital toolkit

FinTech is huge business nowadays, and there are literally hundreds of apps and websites that can help you in your quest for financial stability. One of the utterly brilliant things about this is that it's taken banking out of the realms of snatched telephone conversations on your lunch break or trips to your branch, both of which are a bit of a pain in the arse, and, perhaps more importantly, far too easy to put off. Having quick and easy access to all of the information I need has been essential to holding myself to account and staying on track – it's far easier to succumb to the temptation of keeping your head in the sand if there are any obstacles between you and those numbers. The rise of this type of technology is also pushing traditional banks to introduce these features, which can only be a good thing.

I haven't tried them all, because I have work to do and children to look after, but I do have a few that I can recommend, and others that you might like to try too. You don't have to declare yourself a disciple of one or other of them right away – find the combination that best suits your needs, and let them help you to stay in control.

Budgeting apps

Budgeting apps have gained huge popularity in the last few years, with new ones popping up all the time. Used correctly and consistently, they can help you to stay in control of your budget without the use of a spreadsheet, and keep track of your spending in real time.

What I use: Money Dashboard (Free)

I've used Money Dashboard since the very beginning. I find the app interface easy to use, and the desktop version is an absolute treasure trove of insights about your spending. You can use it to set budgets for specific spending categories, and then keep track of how well you're doing by tagging your transactions as you go along. It also shows all of your account balances in one place, so that you don't have to ping from app to app if you have multiple accounts to keep track of. One of the things I really like is that it gives you a net balance, which factors in any debt, any savings and whatever you have in your current account. A great motivator for anybody trying to achieve a net positive status.

Similar apps available:

- Emma (Free to download, in-app purchases available)
- Yolt (Free)
- Tandem (Free)

As I said, I could probably fill a book just with app recommendations alone, as there are an awful lot of them. Most are free to download, so you can check out their interface and functions and see what works for you.

App-based banking

You probably use a banking app already – most traditional banks have them, although you may not be able to access all functions and it can be frustrating to have to log in to your online banking on a desktop instead. The difference with the new wave of banks is that they are digital only, so you can do absolutely everything in-app. Most also feature tools to help you budget, and you can use them either independently or in conjunction with a budgeting app – the difference being that when you open an account with one of the following providers, it is an actual bank account. It will show up on your credit report, and functions in more or less the exact same way as a traditional current account. A few you could try are:

Monzo

Monzo has burst on to the scene in the last couple of years, heavily targeting millennials with pithy marketing copy and a bright coral aesthetic. The app has lots of different useful tools, such as easy access savings pots and a spending tracker, and joint accounts are available. You receive notifications each time you spend on your card, and your balance updates immediately.

Starling

Starling is similar to Monzo, but sells itself as the banking app that's best for business owners, or people who travel a lot. You can open a personal, business, joint or euro account.

Revolut

Revolut covers the same functions as Starling and Monzo, with emphasis on cheap and easy spending abroad. As someone who has overspent on almost every trip abroad I've taken, usually without being aware of the consequences for weeks afterwards, I think that transparency and reasonable fees are absolutely vital for anyone who likes to travel, or has to for work.

Credit score providers

It took weeks before I was brave enough to look at my credit score. I used to think of it as a mark out of ten for how well I was doing in life, and I knew that it was low. But I've learned that your credit score really is just one element of your financial circumstances and while, yes, improving your score is import-ant if you're looking at applying for a mortgage or similar, it's not the be all and end all.

There are three main credit reporting agencies: Experian, Equifax and Transunion, and each has a different scoring system. The criteria for improving or damaging your score are slightly different for each too – in theory, you can score well with one provider and poorly with another, based on the same data. Even more reason to take your overall score with a pinch of salt – and remember, if your score is low, it can and will be improved as you progress on your journey.

I check my scores on a monthly basis with each of these three providers, and during the time I've been doing so they have gone up and down like yoyos, but the overall trend is positive. That's what you're looking for. Confusingly, the best way to access the information gathered by these credit agencies is often not directly through the agencies themselves. To get the full picture from Equifax, Experian or Transunion, you will usually need to pay a monthly fee. This is not necessary – you can get all the information you need from the third-party services listed below.

Important: the following services also act as credit brokers, and WILL advertise credit products to you. This can be useful, as it may alert you to interest free offers that will allow you to pay off any debt quicker and more cheaply, but please exercise caution.

- **Clearscore (Equifax)**
  You can download the Clearscore app in order to see an overall picture of your current financial outlook, as well as a report that shows changes over the months so that you can track your progress. It scores you out of 700.

- **Credit Karma (Transunion)**
  The Credit Karma app is absolutely full of information, including an in-depth breakdown of each and every one of your credit accounts, with details of how your limit, your balance and your monthly payments have changed over time. It scores you out of 750.

- **Experian (Use the moneysavingexpert.com Credit Club)**
  You can get a very basic version of your Experian score,
  which is basically just a number and little else, for free
  direct from them. But if you'd like a little more guidance,
  you can join the moneysavingexpert.com Credit Club.
  Experian scores are out of 999.

I keep all of my digital tools in a 'money' folder on my phone,
and the easy access that it gives me has enabled me to get into
the habit of checking my balances on a daily basis, and keeping
up to date with my credit score. I no longer live in fear of
accidentally pressing the 'cash and on-screen balance' button
at the cashpoint, or of receiving a bill that has to be paid by
BACS – because I know the lay of the land. This visibility is an
absolute gift, and has definitely been the key to ongoing peace
of mind for me.

Approaches to paying off debt

If you have debt, there are a number of different approaches
that you could take, and what works for you will be different
from what works for someone else, with different circumstances
and different priorities. If you only have one creditor, your
path to solvency is fairly straightforward, but if you have a
number of different accounts, it can be difficult to know how
to distribute the money you've decided to use for repayments.
When I first started the process of getting myself back on track,
I had seven different credit cards, a Nextpay account and a car

on finance. I didn't even know the interest rates on most of them, let alone which I should make a priority.

The language out there can be a little confusing, particularly amongst the Debt Free Community on Instagram, where terms from American debt guru Dave Ramsey's books – like 'Debt Snowball' and 'Baby Steps' – are commonly used. But, in essence, if you want to take a structured approach to paying off debt, there are three ways that you can go about things.

- Pay off in order of interest, from highest to lowest
- Pay off in order of balance, from smallest to largest
- Make fixed payments on all of your accounts

Highest interest first

The first of these, sometimes known as the 'Debt Avalanche', is the one that makes the most logical financial sense. If you set about paying off your debt by focussing on the account with the highest interest first, you will minimize the amount of interest you pay overall, so if that's a priority for you, this is probably your method.

In order to follow this plan, you first need to list your debts in order of interest rate, from highest to lowest. You then pay the minimum amount on all of your balances apart from the one with the highest interest. Here, you allocate everything that's left over from your repayment budget. Once this debt is paid off, you re-allocate your monthly payment to the debt with the next biggest interest, in addition to the minimum amount. And so on and so forth, until everything is paid off.

So, if you had decided you could allocate £1,000 per month for repayments, your plan might look like this* (apologies, a tiny bit of maths here):

£1,000 – (£232.80 + £126.00 + £70.20 + £35.66 + £10.45) = £524.89

Account	Balance	Interest	Minimum Payment	Repayment
Card 1	£1691.39	26.45%	£51.58	£524.89
Card 2	£2796.55	22.8%	£126.00	£126.00
Card 3	£9079.88	19.5%	£232.80	£232.80
Card 4	£2378.72	18.9%	£70.20	£70.20
Card 5	£3565.76	0%	£35.66	£35.66
Card 6	£417.85	0%	£10.45	£10.45

* These are real numbers from my own credit cards as they stand while I write this, so that you can see how this kind of thing works in reality. How much you decide to allocate to repayments is absolutely up to you – this might seem low to some and high to others. It's all relative.

The thing to consider when taking this approach is that you may be left waiting a while for your first 'win' in the form of clearing a balance, especially if your highest interest debt is also your largest amount. Repaying debt can feel like a slog, and if you don't see much impact of your actions for too long, it can be demotivating.

Smallest balance first

This method is the darling of the Debt Free Community – the 'Debt Snowball'. The theory behind it is that, while you will end up paying a little more interest than you would with the previous method, you're more likely to stick to it. That's because if you begin with your smallest debt, you will clear it quicker, thus 'rewarding' you for your efforts and keeping you motivated.

Apart from the order, it works in the exact same way as the highest interest first method – you pay off your first debt, then re-allocate that monthly repayment to your next priority and continue in the same vein until you reach zero. Here's how your plan would differ from the first method, if you had the same amount to pay towards debt:

£1,000 – (£51.58 + £70.20 + £35.66 + £126 + £232.80) = £483.76

Account	Balance	Interest	Minimum Payment	Repayment
Card 1	£417.85	0%	£10.45	£483.76
Card 2	£1691.39	26.45%	£51.58	£51.58
Card 3	£2378.72	18.9%	£70.20	£70.20
Card 4	£2796.55	22.9%	£126.00	£126.00
Card 5	£3565.76	0%	£35.66	£35.66
Card 6	£9079.88	19.5%	£232.80	£232.80

Apart from the fact that you might end up paying more interest overall, something to think about if using this approach is that while you pay off your smaller balances, your larger ones will still be looming over you. It may be that once you make your plan and know that you're on course, this doesn't bother you, but if the thought of saving the worst until last doesn't appeal to you, this probably isn't the method for you.

Fixed payments

This might be the method that makes the least logical sense, but hear me out, because it's the one I use. Something that isn't really taken into account by the first methods is the anxiety that can plague you when you only make the minimum repayments on an account. There's usually a note at the top of your statement, warning you against making only the lowest payment, and it makes me feel squirmy and uncomfortable. Making only the minimum repayment on any of my accounts makes me feel like I've dropped a ball somewhere and, while I'm pretty much okay with it on interest-free balances, I decided more or less from the off that I would be more comfortable making fixed payments. So, the payments that I make are weighted towards my highest interest accounts, but I pay over the minimum amount on all of them.

Account	Balance	Interest	Minimum Payment	Repayment
Card 1	£9079.88	19.5%	£232.80	£300.00
Card 2	£2796.55	22.9%	£126.00	£126.00
Card 3	£1691.39	26.45%	£51.58	£60.00
Card 4	£2378.72	18.9%	£70.20	£100.00
Card 5	£3565.76	0%	£35.66	£50.00
Card 6	£417.85	0%	£10.45	£20.00

If you choose this method, you'll need to decide which your priority debts are and divide your repayment budget accordingly. To give an example, my current priorities are to clear card 2 (American Express), because the interest rate is pretty high and I don't find their team particularly helpful or supportive, and also to reduce the balance on my card 1 (Barclaycard), because it's my highest and it makes me feel a bit anxious.

I've had people question me on this method before, and I'm happy to concede that it probably doesn't make sense to some people. But this is about what makes sense to *you* – it's about giving *you* the best chance of seeing this through and achieving the financial freedom you've been longing for. If you need a bespoke approach to get there, then do that.

A note on 0% balance transfers:

If you're fortunate (or sensible) enough not to have a credit rating resembling poor Marvin from *Pulp Fiction*, like me, you might be able to find a decent balance transfer, which will enable you to shift your balance – or some of it at least – to a card with 0% interest. This can be an absolute game-changer if you're paying a hefty rate, as suddenly all of that cash that was being siphoned off by your lender is now being chipped off your balance instead. You can apply for these directly, or using a website like Martin Lewis's Moneysavingexpert.com. The benefit of the latter is that it allows you to compare rate, length of offer and fees, and to check your eligibility before you apply, so that you're less likely to be turned down, which affects your credit score.

Once you've made the transfer, you can divide the balance on the new interest-free card by the number of months of 0% you've been offered, and that will give you the monthly repayment you need to make in order to clear the account within the interest-free period. Some of these offers come with eye-watering standard interest rates when your offer expires, so it's worth being mindful of this too.

A word of caution, though. At the height of my spending problem, when my head was so deep in the sand that only my feet were visible, I used and abused this tool to basically get hold of as much interest-free credit as possible. Now, hopefully if you've read the rest of this book, you're in the right frame of mind to use this tool as was intended – but if at any point that generous interest free allowance starts looking like an invitation to overspend, step away from the computer (or probably your phone, let's be honest) and recalibrate.

This is, without a doubt, the most admin-heavy part of this process. It takes time, organization and self-awareness to create a set of goals, a budget and a plan to save or pay off debt (or both), but those elements form the blueprint for your path to a better relationship with money – one where you are in control. Now that you have everything you need set up, you're ready to start seeing it through. To start building the new habits that will change your life, and tracking your progress as you make positive changes.

Nine
Time for Change

Now that you're all set up, this is it. Time to start. You might be chomping at the bit, or you might feel a little apprehensive about how you'll manage with the changes you'll be making to your lifestyle. You might be feeling a sort of odd combination of both. All of these feelings are completely normal, and absolutely fine.

When we first started living to a budget, I found myself agonising overspending by the smallest amount. Worried that I would accidentally blow the budget on which I was pinning all my hopes of a stable future, I avoided any situation that would require me to spend money. I put a lot of pressure on myself to get it right from the very beginning, but quickly realized that adjusting to living within your means is a huge learning curve. It's okay to take a little time to work things out, to find your feet. It's a big adjustment.

It's a marathon, not a sprint

Having grown up with a father who dragged us up hill and down dale for most of our childhood, I find climbing a mountain a useful thing to visualize here. There are absolutely no mountains that have a single path going straight up, with check points every few hundred metres. Most of them have multiple paths, and they wind back and forth, with places to stop and rest, and places where we can choose to take a more challenging shortcut every now and again, if we feel up to it.

The same goes for achieving saving goals or paying off debt. We can choose how steeply we want to climb, when to push on and when to rest. I cannot emphasize enough how important this is to your financial, emotional and mental health. Competing and comparing ourselves with others in terms of how quickly we can pay off debt is just as toxic as the comparison we covered earlier; it makes us feel inadequate, makes us push ourselves too hard, makes us burn out. Remember that this is a journey towards financial freedom, not a race to see who can get there first.

Sticking to your budget

Arguably, setting the budget is the easy part. Sticking to it is a different story. We've all done it in the past with everything from Christmas shopping to nights out – set ourselves an amount that we're allowed to spend, then woken up with a burning head and credit card receipts for shots of tequila stuffed in every pocket, or spotted the gift to end all gifts for someone we love and ended up blowing the budget. Eventually, keeping to a set amount of spending every month becomes habitual, but at first it can seem impossible.

One thing that is absolutely essential to adhering to any kind of spending plan is the ability to set boundaries, with both yourself and with others. I've always had a tendency to overpromise and under-deliver – not because I'm lazy or careless, but because I always overestimate my own personal resources, and I hate to let people down. I am naturally terrible at saying no, and turning down invitations or opting out of experiences has always been something that I've struggled with. But developing the ability to set boundaries according to what will protect your wellbeing, both now and in the future, is absolutely essential to being able to stick to any kind of budget that you might have set for yourself. Self-discipline is often easy in the absence of persuasive external forces, like pressure from your peers or incessant marketing, but if you're not equipped to say no to things that will distract you from your goals, it's easy to get derailed.

If I have always been awful at saying no, I've been even worse at doing things in moderation. It's that perfectionism again – when I do something, I want to do it right, and you can see the evidence of that painted all over my credit history. My wedding, birthdays, Christmases, furnishing our house – all evidence of my unwillingness to compromise. But all-or-nothing is not a good attitude to have when it comes to money, as we've already (hopefully) established, and I have had to learn that the only way I will ever be able to reach my financial goals is by managing my own expectations, and accepting that sometimes compromise is necessary – that you don't have to have it all, all at once.

So, an ability to respect your own boundaries, and a willingness to compromise – to accept that you will only be able to do what is financially feasible, rather than the ideal situation you might have been envisaging – are key factors in sticking to your budget. Hopefully, the chapters discussing comparison, relationships and expectation have helped you to understand your feelings on this, but it's worth flipping back to them if and when you start to feel overwhelmed with what can seem like a constant battle between life and budget.

Tracking your progress and staying accountable

One of the very handy, if slightly nail-biting, things about having tens of thousands of people following your progress, is that you can't help but be motivated by it. The main reason I set up the account in the first place was to keep myself accountable and to stop myself from giving up when things got difficult, but I never could have imagined what it would have become. I am buoyed by the support that I receive whenever I post an update, and that, in turn, motivates me more – it's a positive feedback system.

There are a number of different ways that you can recreate that same warm and fuzzy feeling without publishing your figures and your feelings online for all to see. Shortly after I started repaying my debt, I came across a visualisation technique that I'd love to share with you: the grid. I'm not talking about Instagram now, but instead, a simple 10 x 10 grid, where each square represents 1% of your debt, and you colour a square in every time you've repaid that amount. If you do happen to follow me on the *@myfrugalyear* account, you'll be able to see my own grid slowly fill with colour over the months. Each of my squares is worth £254.38, and I pencil them in with care every month – I can't wait to see it finished. There's something about the fact that you can't rub out coloured pencil or felt tip pen that acts as a bit of a deterrent to pushing the 'fuck it' button, and the thought of it sitting at the back of my diary, forever incomplete is a bit sad. It works in the same way for paying off debt and saving for something – if using for saving, just divide your goal by 100 and colour in the squares as you accumulate.

I've included one here, if you'd like to give it a go:

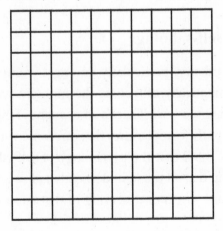

My main recommendation when it comes to staying account-able is to keep it firm, but positive. It's absolutely fine – essential, actually – to examine the reasons why you might have spent over your budget, or not managed to save as much as you wanted to, in order to try and stop that happening in the future. What's not ideal is to confuse making yourself accountable and accepting responsibility for any mistakes with admonishing yourself, or viewing yourself as a failure. Instead of letting that voice in your head attack you, con-verse with it. When it asks you, 'why the fuck can't you just DO this?', respond with, 'yes, you're right – what's holding me back?'

Don't let shame start to creep back in and tell you what to do – it can feel like a battle at first, but over time that voice of reason and self-compassion does get stronger. You get more resilient, and more able to identify and correct slip-ups without beating yourself up.

A note on self-sabotage

There is a tendency, particularly amongst women, to throw ourselves dramatically off course the moment we sense that things are going too well. There's an element of this that could be attributed to the complacency that can come with consistent success, but I think that the psychology of self-sabotage goes far deeper than that – I think, underneath it all, a lot of us don't feel that we are worth or deserving of that success. Once we see ourselves beginning to succeed at making real life changes, we might start to question whether or not we're capable of maintaining them – whether we're good enough. We see ourselves as an imposter in this new way of life, especially if we allow ourselves to dwell on any previous attitudes or patterns of behaviour that we're not particularly proud of. When we've spent so long believing and reinforcing negative ideas about our ability to manage our finances, when we've declared ourselves to be 'bad with money' so many times, when those beliefs are so deeply ingrained in our own concept of our identity, it's difficult to accept that lasting change is possible.

This is why it's absolutely vital that we stop defining ourselves by our financial position, and learn to separate our actions from who we are. If we can't do that, we'll always feel like that person who overspent, or never checked their balance, or didn't save when they could have, represents our true self – and that failure is inevitable. I think it's this that fuels the self-sabotage, and leads us to trip ourselves up when we feel things are going too well. What I hope, is that this book has set the wheels in motion for you to start believing in and trusting yourself. That you can start to see the reasons why things haven't been going to plan, and accept that none of those reasons are to do with who you are as a person. That change is possible, and there's no need for you to sabotage yourself.

Ten

Learning to Find Joy in the In-between

Often, when we set ourselves ambitious goals, we forget that the time between now and then is just as valuable as the time we will have after. Life doesn't begin when we are debt-free, when we buy a house or when we can afford a Destinology holiday. An unwillingness to accept that life can be good – really, really good – without everything needing to be perfect, has held me back for my whole life. It's the reason that I have debt in the first place. But I am determined not to let it get in the way now.

I've written before about 'the slog' – the time while you're paying off debt, when your disposable income is virtually nothing, and the numbers don't seem to be reducing fast enough. Keeping track of every penny can be exhausting, and the highs and lows can leave you feeling emotionally drained. But it is so, so important to find things to enjoy in this time, because you simply cannot just put life on hold until you're in a better financial position, or you've reached that savings goal. Life is far, far too short.

The art of gentle frugality

Here's the thing – I don't think that anybody on the outside, looking in, would necessarily describe my lifestyle as particularly frugal. The word itself can tend to carry with it connotations of meanness, or sparseness, but frugality doesn't have to be either of those things. It's taken a while to find the right balance, but most of the changes we've made as a family, and that I've made as an individual, have actually made life fuller and more enjoyable. We're encouraged to think of being sensible with money as synonymous with being boring – and I certainly bought into that definition for a long time – but it just isn't the case. Reducing our spending and gaining control of our finances doesn't always have to be about cutting back or stripping out – it can be about replacing habits that are driven by consumption with simpler pleasures. It can be about getting back to basics, and rediscovering the joy of making, growing and mending things.

Since beginning this journey, I have found that there are a multitude of unexpected pleasures that come along with consuming less and spending more carefully. Some stem from being able to appreciate things more, some from learning new skills, and some from having honest conversations. Here are a few realizations that I'd like to pass on:

Newness isn't everything

The allure of something shiny and new has always been strong for me. I love the slightly stiff feeling of unworn fabric, and the snap of the swing tag declaring to the world that it's all yours now. New things are exciting and full of promise: the crisp pages of a new diary promising a fresh start, the silky stretch of luxury gym leggings for that better version of you – the one that goes running. It's tantalizing and, until recently, I found it impossible to resist.

But something happened to me. About six months ago, I happened upon a pair of five-year-old floral canvas Dr Martens that I'd tossed to the back of my wardrobe when one of the laces broke. I cleaned them. I put some new laces in. I put them on. I fell in love all over again. The joy that I got from that very minor restoration project outweighed anything I've experienced from a frenzied Asos order. I still get a little buzz when I lace them up. I started looking at other tired items in my wardrobe, and finding out ways that I could reinvigorate them, or give them a second life as something else. I mended dresses with rips, and I dyed faded jeans. Where previously I would have thrown away an old pair of pyjamas without a second thought, I turned my favourites (Teenage Mutant Ninja Turtles, for anyone who's interested) into reusable surface wipes. It was fun, it felt good and, perhaps most satisfyingly, there was no credit card bill at the end.

I've also discovered the absolute thrill of shopping second hand. If you're someone who likes a challenge, trying to find that dress you wanted – in your size – on any number of preloved websites is a thoroughly enjoyable undertaking. Getting something that you were always going to buy at a fraction of the cost is one thing, but there is also the fact that you could probably break even by selling it on at a later date. Plus, it's far more eco-friendly, but we'll come on to that in a moment.

You don't have to resent the things you bought with credit

When I first faced up to what I owed, I could hardly bear to be in the same room as anything I'd bought on a credit card. My possessions seemed to divide themselves into two camps – the 'good' things that I'd bought outright or been given as a gift, and the 'bad' things that had added to my debt. The pale grey, pure-wool rug that was now covered in Weetabix, the clothes I dressed my baby in, the dress I wore the night before my wedding . . . all tainted with the same regret. As I began to come to terms with the debt, and to understand my feelings about it a little better, though, my attitude began to shift. No, I wouldn't buy those things now, unless I could afford to pay cash. No, they weren't really worth it. But by letting them become a physical symbol of my debt shame, what was I gaining?

So, I decided to sell what I no longer liked or had use for, and learn to enjoy the rest. The Weetabix rug is cosy and warm, and big enough to cover most of the uneven floorboards. The baby clothes have been well taken care of, and passed on to the baby of a very dear friend. The dress is one of my favourites, and I wear it whenever the opportunity arises, with thick tights, boots and a jumper. A lot of the things I sold, mainly just to get them out of the way, fetched far more than I was expecting, and I was able to put those funds straight towards my debt. I like the fact that somebody else will get to enjoy them for what they are, with no idea of their legacy.

Saving the planet can be your motivation

As we become more and more aware of the climate crisis, opting out of rampant consumerism seems more and more appealing. The toll that the fast-fashion industry has taken on the planet in just a few decades is enough to shock even the most dedicated Boohoo shopper, and a desire to curb our single-use plastic habits are seeing more of us ditch things like bottled water in favour of refillable bottles.

Many of the changes we can make in order to be kinder to the planet are also kinder to our pockets. In a recent episode of *The Guilty Feminist* podcast, Helen Clarkson, CEO of The Climate Group, identified limiting our air travel and eating less meat as two of the most important changes we can make on an individual level,[1] both of which are more wallet friendly too. The third is not having children – I can attest to the fact that this also saves A LOT of cash, but it's a little too late if you've already got them.

While limiting our consumption for financial reasons can sometimes feel like a drag, a wish to consume less for environmental reasons is generally seen as a good thing, and can help us put a positive spin on spending less. It's okay to be motivated by both, and I find that the two co-exist very well indeed. In trying to better understand my relationship with money, I have been forced to address the fact that I tend to put far too much value on things when I'm coveting them, and far too little once I possess them. Often, in the past, once something is mine it has become boring, disposable, but no more. I have vowed to take better care of the things that I own, in order to prolong their life and reduce the amount that I am buying and throwing away.

Experiences are better than possessions

Now, focussing on experiences is not automatically going to help you to control your spending – take it from someone who is still paying off a meal at Restaurant Sat Bains (two Michelin stars) – but I've found that I regret spending on experiences less. In learning to be less materialistic, I have been able to appreciate the value of experiences more, and they don't tend to fuel the emotional spending cycle for me in the same way that new possessions do.

Experiences are things to be planned in advance, looked forward to, savoured and appreciated. They won't clutter up your living room, or shrink on their first wash.

You can have an impact on others

Perhaps the most delightful surprise of this whole process has been seeing the power of opening up in influencing other people – in the right way. I'm not just talking about sharing my experience online here, although every message I get from someone who feels any level of relief or comfort from my writing still gives me a happy little flutter in my chest. I'm talking about the change I've seen in people in my everyday life. I have friends who are far more open about their money situation since I started speaking about mine, and the relief as we unburden ourselves in those conversations, as we each see that we're not the only ones, is incredible. In explaining exactly why my relationship with money is so difficult, I've seen relatives soften in their attitudes towards others who struggle with their finances. My mum, who taught me everything I know about going shopping, has started making her own string shopping bags and beeswax wraps, for crying out loud.

A word of caution: thrifty is the new black

Minimalism, eco-friendly practice and frugal living have taken on a life of their own in recent years, especially on social media. The Marie Kondo effect has meant that more and more of us are ransacking our homes in search of things that 'spark joy' and feeling the pressure to create neutral, stylish capsule wardrobes, while there is a growing fetishism around 'no-spend' days, weeks, months and even years. While it's good to see this resistance to the incessant wave of consumerism, we run the risk of putting a whole new kind of pressure on ourselves. Even as we resolve to possess less and spend less, we can find ourselves being sold things to kick-start this new lifestyle – from storage boxes and refillable containers to budget planners and cash envelopes.

When it comes to being environmentally conscious, we all owe it to ourselves and to each other to do our best – but that doesn't necessitate amber glass bottles and a label maker. Using what you have is a fundamental principle of both eco-friendliness and frugality – don't forget that.

Special occasions

If there is one thing that will always threaten to jeopardize any good intentions you have, it's a special occasion. Society tells us that we're mean if we try to apply a budget to times of celebration, that anything other than complete excess is unacceptable. If, like me, you find the thought of disappointing anyone you care about absolutely toe-curling, this can be really difficult to navigate. It is often our own expectations of how things should be, fuelled by hours of scrolling social media, that threaten to derail us the most.

As with most things to do with expectation, though, being honest often helps a great deal. If we are able to be open and realistic about what we can and can't afford to spend on special occasions, we don't run the risk of letting anyone down at a later point. Planning for these times well in advance, whether that means putting money aside for expensive events or simply having a conversation about how much we are able to participate, is vital. It is usually when we wing it that we find ourselves in deep water.

Have a mindful Christmas

As I write this, the run up to Christmas has well and truly begun, and the expectation is being laid on thick. I went into November with a solid plan and a modest budget, and already I can feel the pressure starting to mount – the fretting about whether my children will be disappointed when they don't wake up to the entire content of the Smyths catalogue, or whether people will think us rude for not sending Christmas cards. But then I think of last Christmas, and what it cost us to fulfil all of those expectations, and I realize that it's just not worth the potential financial impact. Some research carried out by mobile app company Wagestream found that people expected to start the year with an average of £252 debt left over from the festive period alone, with shift and gig workers putting £352 of festive spending on credit. Respondents told researchers they feared they would not be able to pay off Christmas debts until May.[2] Christmas is wonderful, but it doesn't warrant spending half of the following year playing catch-up.

Marketers start from as early as August, slowly feeding us the idea of a perfect Christmas that almost never stacks up to reality. We all know, logically, that nobody's Christmas Day is ever perfect; whoever's cooking the dinner will get stressed, siblings will fight and someone will get a bit too pissed. But somehow, advertisers are able to convince us to suspend reality as we shop, and open our wallets with the conviction that all of the stress will simply melt away if we can just stage the perfect scene: perfect decorations, mountains of presents, mouth-watering food.

We can resist this, though, if we try to remember what it is that we really love most about the festive season – what really makes it all magical. There are so many Christmassy things that don't have to cost a fortune – driving round to see the lights, baking, even sticking cloves into oranges, for some reason. You can move the focus of the season from volume of gifts to quality-time spent together, and create new traditions for the future.

Birthday pressure

My eldest son's birthday is Christmas Eve, and, until last year, it always just got a bit lost in among the Christmas celebrations. When he turned four, we decided that we really wanted to throw him a proper birthday party – so we did. We hired entertainers and a church hall and bought food and drink, and it cost us a small fortune that we just didn't have. On the day of the party, we had to borrow £20 from a relative for the key deposit, because we had absolutely no access to cash – I was planning to see through the rest of the month on a credit card. It should have been lovely, watching him surrounded by his friends, having the time of his life, and on one level it was. But I was completely preoccupied with the panic of not having been able to withdraw £20 from my account, and it sucked all of the joy out of what should have been a special occasion for us all. I remember thinking then that things needed to change, but it took another three months of moments like that before I finally bit the bullet.

Our youngest son's first birthday was in the summer, post wake-up call, and our approach to it couldn't have been more different. We bought him minimal presents, and had a low-key family picnic in the park. It was lovely.

Two steps forward, one step back

The only way to succeed with improving our finances long term, and resisting the urge to give up at the first hurdle, is to understand that success is not a straight line. Over the summer, we had some car troubles that meant we had to temporarily add to our debt, and it stung. When you've worked so hard to chip away at your debt, only to watch it reappear at lightning speed with a shake of the head from your mechanic, it can feel like there's no point in trying.

In some ways, I'm grateful that our first experience of taking a backwards step came so soon in the process, because it taught me early on that setbacks don't have to mean the end of your journey. And once you know that – once you know that you can get back on track even when life throws you a curveball – it gives you absolute confidence in your ability to do this.

'Rest' when you need to

Sometimes the thing that threatens to throw you off course isn't an unexpected bill or a drop in income. Sometimes it's just fatigue. Paying off debt can feel never-ending and unrewarding, and living within your means while they are limited by repayments can be dull and exhausting.

I'm going to tell you a secret: it's okay if you need a break. It's okay if you need to slow down, and go down to minimum repayments for a couple of months to give yourself some breathing space. Yes, it will mean delaying your goals a little, but it's better than giving up altogether. If you're feeling jaded, or like you're on the verge of throwing in the towel, I urge you to take a break – but plan it in, and make sure that you get back on track as soon as you feel able. You are in control now – you've got this.

Self-care is not a £75 facial

Well, sometimes it is. But most of the time, self-care is as simple as reconnecting with some very basic needs. Generally, if you can make time to take care of those, the aforementioned facial serves as a nice treat, rather than something you booked with your credit card at 11.48 p.m., tired and frustrated after finishing work, cooking dinner, washing up, and, crucially, missing the window to wash your hair and do a £3 face mask. Again.

'I just want something for ME!' you scream internally as you furiously tap those digits in, not really giving a flying fuck about the extra you'll have to pay out from an already tight budget next month – because you deserve it. When you're going through a stressful time, whether it's because of money or for some other reason, it's even more important to make sure that you take care of yourself, and most of that is to do with ringfencing some time to rebalance. As women, we tend to be very good at making sure everyone else's needs are met, and ignore our own until we're quite literally on our arses.

Boundaries are the bedrock of self-care. If you can draw a line around certain times in your day, and make sure you are able to take a few extra minutes to think about how you're feeling, to consider what you need, you won't need that facial. Sometimes self-care is drinking a glass of water, or taking some extra time in the shower, or listening to a podcast and really paying attention to the words. Of course, there are times when a proper pamper is lovely – but it won't help if the basics aren't covered. The truth is that, for the most part, looking after ourselves is free, or costs very little. For most of us, it's only when we start to feel neglected that things get expensive.

How to 'treat yo'self' without breaking the bank

A somewhat surprising aspect of getting a hold on my finances has been its effect on my attitude towards 'treats'. While I was battling growing debt and declining self-worth, everything I bought for myself was treated as an undeserved, guilty secret. The smallest thing felt like an overindulgence, and after a while I was unable to differentiate between a small pick-me-up and a complete *Parks-and-Recreation*-style blowout. They felt like the same thing.

Since gaining more clarity and control, I have been able, in a couple of instances, to buy something for myself without guilt. I'd forgotten what that felt like.

It you're struggling to find ways to spend on yourself without losing perspective or control, I'd recommend planning your treats ahead of time, and making sure that you set a clear limit on how much you're willing to spend – then sticking to it. In doing this, you'll learn to trust yourself that bit more, and future treats won't feel like quite such a threat.

A note on generosity

Over the course of the last few months, I have found that it's actually rarely the things that I want for myself that threaten to throw a spanner in the works. A huge part of my spending problem has been buying out of some misguided sense that you have to be generous with material things in order to show someone you care, or to be well-liked. I've always been an extravagant gift buyer – I get it from my mum. I like to think that I also share her ability to choose just the right thing, but the reality is that sometimes you actually can't afford 'just the right thing' – and that's okay. My tendency to go overboard when it comes to gestures of love, friendship or admiration, I think, stems from a feeling that those things are not, in themselves, enough. That *I* am not enough.

Generosity of spirit is a wonderful quality, when it comes from a place of genuine kindness, and I aim to always be generous in life. But being generous and thoughtful doesn't have to be about material things. You can be generous with your words, or your attention, or your time.

Eleven
A Beginning, Not the End

I will always find it ironic how being anonymous enabled me to finally be my authentic self online, and consequently to be more honest in real life. Once I realized I wasn't the only one struggling with the daily realities of managing my money, I was finally able to stop pretending, to stop trying to live up to what I thought everyone else's expectations of me were, and just be real. It has been that new ability to examine what I really think, feel and find important, to look my shame defiantly in the eye, and to accept my flaws, that has enabled me to let go of my negative money habits and start to build new, better ones. Habits that are based on what's going on in my day to day life, as well as being designed to help me meet my long-term goals.

I've always felt held back by my financial situation, in both practical and psychological terms. The effect of money worries on your self-worth can be crippling, and that cycle of paying off debt and then being forced by circumstance to accrue it again can make you feel like you're trapped in a giant hamster wheel, without a clue how to get off. You're exhausted, but you can't stop. You feel like you're trying to move forward, but it keeps bringing you back in a circle. This book is not a three-point plan for success, or a guide to the quickest way to pay off debt or save for a deposit, but I think it might help you to step off the wheel and take control of the direction of your own future.

Once we're free of the burden of financial shame – even before we've achieved our money goals – it's amazing what we can achieve. I am literally writing this book because, after years of chasing my tail, beating myself up and burying my head in the sand, I managed to find another path. I have spoken to others who have finally found the confidence to apply for new jobs, change careers or end toxic relationships after taking hold of their finances and letting go of that same baggage. Even just the catharsis of opening up – of talking about it, or writing it down – can open our minds to new possibilities.

A promise

So, there it is. There is no single diagnosis or prescription for our financial difficulties, no magical cure, because each and every one of us has a relationship with money that is as unique and complicated as a fingerprint. We each have our own journey ahead of us, our own decisions to make, our own lives to continue to build. We all have different pasts, different circumstances and different priorities.

With that in mind, what I hope this book has given you is some insight into your relationship with money and the effect that it has on the rest of your life. I hope it has encouraged you to ask yourself some questions, and that you have given yourself time and space to reflect on the answers. I hope it has shown you that you have the power to change, and given you the confidence and the tools to do so. I hope it has made you feel more positive about the future, because there is absolutely no reason why, with the right mindset and the right help, you can't go on to achieve freedom from your financial demons.

If we are to achieve a healthy and balanced relationship with money, we need to get to a place where we trust ourselves to make the right decisions, but know that we are also capable of handling any mistakes we might make along the way. There will be ups and downs. There may be windfalls and pay rises. There may be redundancies and illness. None of us know what is just around the corner, but once we have this under control, once we have a plan, we can navigate any bend in the river.

It's never too late to start making positive changes. It may be the case that we have to do a little excavation in order to re-lay our foundations, to form new habits and let go of old hang-ups, and that can be painful, but it is so, so worth it. If we can rewrite our relationship with money, stop using it as an emotional crutch and develop new, healthier coping strategies, we can open the door to a brighter future. We have to learn to separate our actions from our identities and accept ourselves for the flawed and complicated, but worthwhile, people that we are. If we can do these things, we can look forward to a new version of our own, real lives – one where we are mentally healthy, emotionally fulfilled and financially secure.

We'll get there, I promise.

Notes

Preface

1   https://www.tuc.org.uk/news/unsecured-debt-hits-new-peak-£15400-household – new-tuc-analysis

1. Broke, Not Poor

1   https://www.youtube.com/watch?v=hD5f8GuNuGQ
2   https://www.stylist.co.uk/long-reads/how-to-manage-money-personal-finances-debt-credit-cards-loans/274332

2. What are We So Ashamed Of?

1   https://www.ted.com/talks/brene_brown_listening_to_shame?language=en
2   https://www.ted.com/talks/brene_brown_listening_to_shame?language=en
3   https://effectiviology.com/ostrich-effect/

4 https://www.ft.com/content/0ae64e5a-ba98-11e9-8a88-aa6628ac896c

5 Holder, *Alex, Open Up: Why Talking About Money Will Change Your Life* (London: Serpent's Tale, 2019)

6 https://www.bbc.co.uk/news/business-45744552

7 https://play.acast.com/s/griefcast

8 http://www.huver.com/Misc_Resources/Windfall%20Nefe.pdf

3. Money on Your Mind

1 https://www.moneyandmentalhealth.org/

2 https://www.moneysavingexpert.com/news/2018/11/more-than-100-000-people-in-problem-debt-attempt-suicide-each-ye/

3 https://www.ted.com/talks/andrew_solomon_depression_the_secret_we_share?language=en

4 https://www.bbc.co.uk/news/business-47693725

5 https://www.moneyandmentalhealth.org/wp-content/uploads/2019/03/debt-mental-health-facts-2019.pdf

6 https://www.psychologytoday.com/gb/blog/science-choice/201806/5-patterns-compulsive-buying

7 https://www.psychologytoday.com/us/blog/science-choice/201801/10-reasons-why-people-spend-too-much

8 https://www.independent.co.uk/life-style/shopping-addiction-recognised-mental-illness-psychologist-a8481046.html

9 https://psychagainstausterity.files.wordpress.com/2015/03/paa-briefing-paper.pdf

10 https://www.psychologytoday.com/gb/blog/two-takes-depression/201709/risk-factors-and-warning-signs-suicide

11 https://www.moneysavingexpert.com/news/2018/11/more-than-100-000-people-in-problem-debt-attempt-suicide-each-ye/

4. Under the Influence

1 https://www.statista.com/chart/16899/social-media-advertising/

2 https://www.independent.co.uk/money/spend-save/social-media-influencers-cost-advert-lifestyle-partnerships-links-debt-a9160766.html

3 https://www.asa.org.uk/uploads/assets/uploaded/3af39c72-76e1-4a59-b2b47e81a034cd1d.pdf

4 https://www.asa.org.uk/uploads/assets/uploaded/e3158f76-ccf2-4e6e-8f51a710b3237c43.pdf

5 https://the-frugality.com

6 Lanier, Jaron, *Ten Arguments for Deleting your Social Media Accounts Right Now* (London: Bodley Head, 2018)

5. Finance is a Feminist Issue

1 https://www.goodmoneyweek.com/facts-and-stats

2 https://www.bloodygoodperiod.com/#intro

3 https://www.ons.gov.uk/employmentandlabourmarket/peopleinwork/earningsandworkinghours/bulletins/genderpaygapintheuk/2019

4 https://www.goodmoneyweek.com/media/press-releases/women-losing-out-pay-rises-because-they-feel-awkward

5   https://www.moneyadviceservice.org.uk/blog/is-debt-more-of-a-female-issue-than-male

6   https://www.independent.co.uk/money/spend-save/international-womens-day-gender-pay-gap-uk-debt-pensions-female-workers-a8813256.html

7   https://www.fawcettsociety.org.uk/

8   https://www.fawcettsociety.org.uk/the-gender-pay-gap-and-pay-discrimination-explainer

9   https://www.itv.com/news/2020-01-10/samira-ahmed-wins-sex-discrimination-equal-pay-claim-against-bbc/

10 https://www.moneywise.co.uk/news/2018-04-27%E2%80%8C%E2%80%8C/quarter-new-parents-get-debt

11 https://www.ons.gov.uk/employmentandlabourmarket/peopleinwork/earningsandworkinghours/bulletins/annualsurveyofhoursandearnings/2019

12 https://pregnantthenscrewed.com/

13 https://pregnantthenscrewed.com/campaigns/

14 https://www.researchandmarkets.com/reports/4416739/weight-loss-and-weight-management-market-by

6. 'Oh, You're Still Renting?'

1   https://www.theguardian.com/money/2017/jun/12/one-in-four-households-in-britain-will-rent-privately-by-end-of-2021-says-report

2   Grillo, Medina, *Home Sweet Rented Home: Transform Your Home Without Losing Your Deposit* (London: Mitchell Beazley, 2019)

7. Into the Black

1   https://motherofalllists.com/2019/05/10/25k-debt-how-i-got-into-it-how-i-am-getting-out-again/
2   https://www.moneydashboard.com/
3   https://www.moneysavingexpert.com/news/2018/02/new-credit-card-rules-to-help-those-in-persistent-debt/
4   https://www.stepchange.org/debt-info/arranging-payment-with-creditors.aspx
5   https://www.satsumaloans.co.uk/payday-loans

8. Getting Ready

1   https://www.moneysavingexpert.com/cheapenergyclub

10. Learning to Find Joy in the In-between

1   https://guiltyfeminist.com/episode/?episode=214
2   https://www.theguardian.com/business/2019/jan/07/average-uk-household-debt-now-stands-at-record-15400

Places to Seek Further Help

While I hope that this book has provided you with the tools that you need to start changing your relationship with money and taking control of your finances, I know that everyone's situation is very different. Addressing your financial situation can feel like opening the world's biggest can of worms, and the emotional labour that comes with it can be completely exhausting. It's absolutely fine – and sometimes essential – to seek some extra guidance:

With debt:

StepChange Debt Charity
https://www.stepchange.org/

Christians Against Poverty
https://capuk.org/

National Debtline
https://www.nationaldebtline.org/

With general money management:

The Money Advice Service
https://www.moneyadviceservice.org.uk/en

MoneySavingExpert.com
https://www.moneysavingexpert.com/

With mental health:

Mind
https://www.mind.org.uk/

The Blurt Foundation
https://www.blurtitout.org/

Samaritans
https://www.samaritans.org/

CALM
https://www.thecalmzone.net/

Other resources:

Citizen's Advice
https://www.citizensadvice.org.uk/

Pregnant Then Screwed
https://pregnantthenscrewed.com/

Further Reading

If any of the topics covered in part one have piqued your interest, and you're keen to read more, here are some good places to start:

The Joseph Rowntree Foundation
https://www.jrf.org.uk/

Psychologists Against Austerity
http://www.psychchange.org/psychologists-against-austerity.html

The Money and Mental Health Policy Institute
https://www.moneyandmentalhealth.org/

The Fawcett Society
https://www.fawcettsociety.org.uk/

Generation Rent
https://www.generationrent.org/

Acknowledgements

I'm not sure that everyone does, but I think I have at least skimmed the acknowledgments of every book I have ever read. They are a little window into the author's world, a peek at the invisible support network holding them up. Never in my wildest dreams did I imagine that I would one day be writing my own, or just how difficult it would be to adequately express my gratitude.

To my agent, Julia Silk, thank you for guiding me so elegantly through my first foray into the world of publishing, for your unyielding enthusiasm and for helping me to keep the imposter syndrome at bay. To my editor, Anna Steadman, thank you for your light touch on the page, for making me laugh with your edit notes and for your calm confidence in this book right from the very beginning.

To everyone who has contributed to this book, thank you for gifting me your words. To everyone who has followed, commented, messaged or engaged with the *@myfrugalyear* Instagram page, thank you for trusting me, an anonymous stranger, with your stories. I owe so much of this to you.

To my two sisters, Chloe and Georgina, thank you for not looking at me like a crazy person when I told you about what was going on, and for always asking how I am – even when I take five working days to respond. To Stef, Lucy, Kathryn, Sam and Hayley, thank you for always listening, never judging, and for making me laugh in a way that my pelvic floor can now barely withstand. Thank you, Jess, for your constant support and positivity, and for allowing me and my book to permeate your newborn bubble.

To my grandparents, thank you for helping me to remember who I am: the girl who knew what a kumquat was, aged five. To Fiona, Pete, Trudi, Brad and Fran, thank you for the many ways in which you have supported our little family throughout the last few years – and me, throughout my entire life.

To Mum, thank you for teaching me what it means to be kind, through your own unending kindness and generosity towards me, and now my children.

To my husband, Phil, thank you for letting me share this part of our story. Thank you for coming on this ridiculous journey with me, for taking it all in your stride. Mostly, thank you for working as hard as you do so that we can build a better future, together.

And finally, in ever loving memory of you, Dad, and your Three Peaks T-shirt.

Index